Proofreading and Revision Guide

The Writer's Craft

A Concise Rhetoric and Handbook

The Writer's Craft

A Concise Rhetoric and Handbook

A. R. Coulthard

Appalachian State University

Wadsworth Publishing Company
A Division of Wadsworth, Inc.
Belmont, California

English Editor: Kevin Howat

Production Editor: Carolyn Tanner

Designer: Rick Chafian

Copy Editor: Don Yoder

Printed in the United States of America

1   2   3   4   5   6   7   8   9   10 — — — 84   83   82   81   80

Library of Congress Cataloging in Publication Data

Coulthard, A. R.
  The writer's craft.

  Includes index.
  1. English language—Rhetoric.   2. English
language—Grammar—1950-   I. Title.
PE1408.C655   808'.042   79-21189
ISBN 0-534-00768-6

Acknowledgments

The student essays "Mighty Minnie," by Kim Dickens, "My Hill," by Marty Begin, "Hunters' Retreat," by David Tolley, and "Goodbye, California," by Suzanne Tise, are all used by permission of the authors. The material on short story analysis in chapter four was originally published in slightly different form in *College Composition and Communication* and is used by permission of the National Council of Teachers of English. The essay "Reflections Upon a Golden Eye" was originally published in slightly different form in *Notes on Contemporary Literature* and is used by
(Continued on page 385)

Contents

Preface

In my approximately two decades of teaching writing, I have witnessed many changes. The devaluing of writing, in spite of the continued lip service our culture pays it, is the most dramatic. Today, writing teachers not only must work harder to motivate students to try to write well, but we must also provide them with more guidance and direction than before.

I began to develop the materials of this book to do just that. In the belief that sound organization is basic to written communication, I try to help students learn to write papers with an orderly sequence of thought. The essays in their readers, however, are often loosely structured and of little use to beginning writers as models of form. As a result, I began to write my own model essays and to collect student writing with an eye to tight structure and clear expression. Many of these essays appear in this book. In a similar fashion, the information on writing about literature was devised to guide my introductory literature students through the special difficulties of literary analysis, and the chapter on research began as an attempt to simplify for young writers material which often is presented in a confusing manner.

Like the Rhetoric, the Handbook is intended as a practical writing guide for modern students. The entries are easy to locate and easy to understand. I have intentionally avoided the overly technical, the esoteric, and the exceptional. Students want quick solutions to their mechanical and grammatical problems, not theoretical discussion.

Clarity, simplicity, and instructing by illustration are the guiding principles of both parts of *The Writer's Craft*. The Rhetoric begins with "The Writing Process," which explains how to plan and shape a paper and presents strategies for selecting a topic, outlining, deciding on tone, and proofreading and editing the final copy.

Chapter 2, "Types of Essays," describes eight common expository forms and the strategies peculiar to each. This chapter offers model essays illustrating form and style and suggests sample topics for student writing.

Chapter 3, "The Research Paper," focuses on strategies for research writing and provides a twelve-step method for completing a research paper. This chapter is modeled on the 1977 *MLA Handbook* style and discusses library use, note-taking, quotations, paraphrases, and plagiarism. This information is presented under the appropriate writing step—that is, at the place in the process where the student is most likely to need it. In addition, the research chapter includes footnote and bibliography models and two sample research papers.

Chapter 4 concludes the Rhetoric with a discussion of writing about literature. Designed for introductory literature classes, where *The Writer's Craft* may be used with an anthology, this chapter gives students basic tips on writing themes on short stories, poems, novels, and plays and provides sample papers on each.

The Handbook contains information on fifty-five common writing errors. These entries are arranged alphabetically for easy access, but students may also use the Proofreading and Revision Guide at the front of the book to help them solve specific problems in organization, unity, development, grammar, style, punctuation, and spelling. All entries are simple and concise, yet sufficiently thorough to enable students to improve their writing in all these areas.

These are some of the outstanding features of *The Writer's Craft:*

Completeness and conciseness. The Rhetoric provides students all the information they need to write eight common types of expository themes, as well as research and literary analysis papers. The Handbook contains all the information found in longer books, but presents it in succinct and accessible form.

Flexibility. The book may be used to instruct the entire class in a particular rhetorical mode before they begin to write, or to provide individual students with information and models after they have determined during the writing process which form best fits their content. Because each form constitutes a self-contained unit, instructors may rearrange the assignments into the order which best suits them. The book may be used alone or with an essay anthology.

Sample essays. The brief sample essays are accessible models of form and clarity on topics of interest to a college audience. Several were written by students. All have beginnings, middles, and ends.

Structured approach to research. Research writing is simplified into a logical twelve-step procedure. This process is reinforced by a separate list of the twelve steps inside the front cover of the book. One of the sample research papers illustrates the shorter form preferred by many teachers.

Concise Handbook entries. Entries are brief and to the point, providing just the information students need to correct their writing problems. Information relevant to literary analysis is a special feature.

Convenient marking symbols. The alphabetized list on the inside of the back cover makes marking symbols easy to locate. Instructors have the choice of using either descriptive symbols or numbers corresponding to the fifty-five Handbook entries. These symbols are keyed to page numbers which quickly direct students to the information needed.

This book is my attempt to demystify the complicated and often confusing process of writing and to respond to the needs of today's students. Writing well has never been easy, and teaching writing in our fast-paced, multimedia age presents a special challenge. Most students, however, can learn to write competently if they are properly directed. *The Writer's Craft* provides this guidance simply and clearly.

Acknowledgments

I wish to thank my family and especially my wife, Lynn, for their patience and understanding during the time this book was in progress. I am grateful to J. A. Rice for editorial assistance, to Sam Terry for classroom-testing my materials, and to my colleagues at Appalachian State University, especially Loyd Hilton and Richard Rupp, for advice and encouragement.

Special thanks go to Nadine Hampton, Janet Wellborn, and Janet Littleton for their generous clerical assistance.

For helpful and considerate criticism, I owe a debt of gratitude to Kevin Howat, Sheryl Fullerton, and Carolyn Tanner of Wadsworth and to Randy Cade, formerly of Wadsworth. Finally, my thanks go to these reviewers whose suggestions were invaluable in improving my manuscript: Stella Bruton of West Chester State College, Susan Cowles of Tallahassee Community College, Paul Doyle of Nassau Community College, Joyce Lipkis of Santa Monica College, and Veronica Muzic of The Williamsport Area Community College.

The Writer's Craft

A Concise Rhetoric and Handbook

The
Rhetoric

1

The Writing Process

Maybe you don't feel like writing and maybe you don't really have anything you want to say, but you are required to produce a paper of five hundred words by Friday. You may even, in addition, be required to write a specific *type* of paper. Under these conditions, certain questions are inevitable: "How do I get started?" "What can I do to make my paper readable?" This chapter attempts to answer those questions and, in so doing, to minimize the insecurity common among writers, especially during the early stages of composition.

The information under "Types of Writing Assignments" will help you produce papers for the two most common assignments. One series of steps is a plan to follow if a certain type of paper is required. (See Chapter 2.) The other outlines a writing plan to use if you are permitted to select the type of organization which best fits the topic you have chosen. Virtually all writing assignments call for one approach or the other.

"Selecting a Topic" gives advice on how to choose interesting subjects which are also suitable to the assignment and length of paper. For additional ideas, you may refer to the sample topics listed for each type of paper in Chapter 2.

After you have decided on a subject, at some stage during the process of composition you must identify the major points of your paper and arrange them in their most effective order. "Outlining" gives instructions on how to formulate a plan for your paper. "Organization," a closely related unit, examines the whole paper, including titles, and offers strategies for composing the beginnings, middles, and ends characteristic of tightly structured expository (informational) writing.

Just as the parts of a paper must be tightly unified, so must its language reflect a consistent attitude. Because you must consider your audience in deciding on a tone, "Tone and Audience" discusses these two matters together and offers advice on selecting the language appropriate to your subject and suitable to a general reading audience.

Finally, "Proofreading and Editing" gives instructions on how to revise, polish, and otherwise fine-tune your finished product so that mechanical, grammatical, and stylistic errors do not detract from your paper's content.

TYPES OF WRITING ASSIGNMENTS

There are two basic types of writing assignments: Either you are told simply to write a paper, or else you are assigned a particular type of paper. Each assignment requires a different strategy.

Writing strategy for free choice of type of paper

1. Choose a topic you know something about and are interested in. This is essential.

2. Begin to write. Don't put it off. The blank page is the writer's greatest fear. Don't worry about grammar, punctuation, style, or organization at this point. Just get some related thoughts down on paper. If you can't get started, list some ideas and then try putting them together.

3. Examine what you have written. Deduce from your first draft the form which best suits your content. (See Chapter 2 for information on common expository forms.)

4. Formulate an outline of main points consistent with the form you have chosen. (See Outlining, p. 7.) Rearrange the parts of the rough draft and put them in their most effective order. Write notes to yourself in the margins. Strike out ideas which don't fit and add details where needed. To be of any use, rough drafts *have* to be messy. Remember that the organization of your paper must be consistent with the form you have chosen.

5. Following your outline and edited rough draft, write a second draft. Don't hesitate to add new details or even to change your plan of organization if necessary.

6. Now carefully proofread and edit what you have written. Read the paper the first time for overall unity and flow of thought. Then read it again, concentrating on the structure, wording, grammar, punctuation, and spelling of each individual sentence. Make all necessary corrections.

7. Carefully copy or type a final version, incorporating all the corrections made on the previous draft.

8. Before turning in the paper, proofread it again and make neat final corrections. If these are extensive, make one last draft.

Writing strategy for assigned type of paper

1. Choose a topic you know something about and are interested in, but which also can be developed in the assigned form. (See Chapter 2.)

2. Begin to write, keeping the form requirements in mind. Don't worry about grammar, punctuation, and style at this point.

3. Formulate an outline of main points consistent with what you have written and with the demands of the assigned form. (See Outlining, p. 7.) Edit and revise your rough draft to fit the form. Strike out and add details as needed.

4. Following your outline and edited rough draft, write a second draft. Don't hesitate to add new ideas and details, but remember that you cannot change the *type* of paper you are writing.

5. Now carefully proofread and edit what you have written. Read the paper the first time for overall unity and flow of thought. Then read it again, concentrating on the structure, wording, grammar, punctuation, and spelling of each individual sentence. Make all necessary corrections.

6. Carefully copy or type a final version, incorporating all the corrections made on the previous draft.

7. Before turning in the paper, proofread it one last time and make neat final corrections. If these are extensive, prepare another draft.

SELECTING A TOPIC

Except in the case of examination essays, teachers seldom tell students exactly what topic to write a paper on. The freedom to choose your own subject should work to your advantage, but some students find that selecting a topic is the most difficult part of the writing process.

Make sure that the topic you select fits the assignment. If a specific type of paper is assigned, you should think only of topics which can be developed in that form. Suppose the assignment is to write a process, or "how-to," paper. In preparing to write this type of essay, you should consider activities you can do well—a hobby, a sport, a special skill, a job you have held. If the assignment is a character sketch, begin your planning by recalling interesting or unusual people you have known. Start thinking about possible topics immediately. You may suffer an attack of writer's block if you put off selecting a subject until you sit down to write.

If the assignment is open—if you are told simply to write a paper—then your choice of topics is much broader. For such an assignment, you may write a "how-to" paper, a character sketch, or another type of essay, or you may wish to write about an idea that has been on your mind or discuss a current issue of personal interest to you—something pertaining to social trends, education, politics, or even campus affairs. Be sure to narrow your subject to a topic which can be handled in the short space of a theme. "Swimming," for instance, is much too broad, but you could explain how to do the jackknife in a brief paper.

Some topics should be avoided, even though they may be of interest to you. Trivial, highly personal subjects such as "Why I Love My Dog" are not likely to result in interesting papers, unless you are capable of treating them with a fresh approach (humorously or satirically, for instance). Nor should you write papers on platitudes like "You can't judge a book by its cover" or "Money can't buy happiness"—again unless you can treat them with an unusual twist ("You *can* judge a book by its cover"). In addition to trite ideas, avoid subjects which have been overworked in the news media and elsewhere, such as abortion and marijuana laws. But don't dodge a topic simply because it is controversial. Controversial issues often make interesting papers. Whatever subject you choose, make your point of view clear and firm. You will not be graded on the stand you take, even on moral issues, but on how well you support your point of view and express your ideas. No subject is taboo if it is handled with good sense and good taste.

In any case, follow this important rule in selecting a topic: *Write about something you know and are interested in.* A writer has no business writing on anything else.

OUTLINING

An outline is a blueprint for an essay and an indispensable aid to organization. Early in the writing process, you must organize your content into some logical form. An outline helps you to do this.

Outlines range in form from the brief topic outline to the elaborate sentence outline, which can be almost as long as the paper itself. Of the two, the topic outline is the more useful. An outline is, after all, a tentative plan. The actual development of a body of thought or information should be done during the writing of the paper and not during the outlining stage. Also keep in mind that an outline is a guide and not a straitjacket. As you write your paper, do not hesitate to adjust and revise your plan if the need arises. It is better to change the blueprint than to construct a lopsided house. Numerous and major deviations from your outline, however, indicate that the topic needs rethinking.

The topic outline can be a skeletal listing of main points only. Suppose you are writing a paper on how to drive a golf ball. If you know the process extremely well, a skeletal outline (the minimal outline a writer can employ) may suffice:

```
             Driving a Golf Ball


Thesis: Learning to drive a golf ball

requires the mastery of five steps.

    I.  Stance

   II.  Grip

  III.  Backswing

   IV.  Downswing

    V.  Follow-through
```

If, however, you need to do more preliminary thinking on your subject, a more detailed outline will be helpful:

```
             Driving a Golf Ball


Thesis: Learning to drive a golf ball

requires the mastery of five steps.
```

I. Stance

    A. Determine place of stance.

    B. Spread feet shoulder's width.

    C. Keep feet parallel, toes pointed straight ahead.

    D. Keep feet flat on ground.

    E. Bend knees slightly.

    F. Bend slightly forward at waist.

II. Grip

    A. Clutch end of grip with left hand.

    B. Place left thumb parallel on grip.

    C. Keep left hand firm but relaxed.

    D. Place bottom of right thumb over left thumb.

    E. Keep right thumb parallel to shaft.

    F. Interlock left forefinger with right little finger.

    G. Grip slightly tighter with right hand.

III. Backswing

    A. Keep eyes on ball.

B. Bring clubhead straight back from ball at moderate speed.

C. Turn hips and shoulders slightly to right.

D. Bend left leg slightly.

E. Keep left arm straight.

F. Allow right arm to bend slightly.

G. Bring hands slightly back of right ear.

H. Keep feet firm.

IV. Downswing

A. Don't hesitate.

B. Bring clubhead straight toward ball.

C. Smoothly increase club speed.

D. Keep left arm stiff.

E. Keep wrists stiff.

F. Allow left-hand grip to tighten.

G. Power with right hand and arm.

H. Straighten out both arms.

I. Shift body weight forward.

V. Follow—through

    A. Keep head down.

    B. Push clubhead "through" ball,
       maintaining club speed.

    C. "Break" wrists.

    D. Allow body to turn slightly toward
       left.

    E. Lean slightly forward, pivoting on
       right foot.

    F. Continue club arc.

    G. Bring club to rest just above left
       shoulder.

Either outline will produce a seven-paragraph theme: an introduction, a separate paragraph describing each of the five steps of the process, and a brief conclusion. Since all essays should have opening and closing paragraphs, the introduction and conclusion are not shown in the outline.

If the outline is workable, the main points may easily be converted into topic sentences. To illustrate, the first major item listed is "I. Stance." The topic sentence of the first paragraph of the body of the essay could be simply "The first step in learning to drive a golf ball is to master the proper stance." In this manner, the paper grows out of the outline, as a tree springs from a seed. The practice of making an outline *after* a paper is written is as absurd as drawing up a house plan after the building has been constructed.

An outline is likely to produce a solid paper if it meets several specific standards. Check your outlines for the following:

1. COMPLETENESS. The main points should cover the topic adequately and deliver what the thesis statement promises.

2. LOGIC.   Each main point should be clearly related to the thesis. If subpoints are stated, each should be logically related to the main point under which it is listed.

3. BALANCE.   All the main points should be generally equal in importance. An outline would be imbalanced, for instance, if "Keep left arm straight" were listed as a main point equal in importance to "Stance" and "Grip."

4. ORDER. The points should be arranged in their most effective sequence. This is relatively easy in a process paper because the steps follow a time order. In other types of papers, however, you will have to decide on the most effective order in which to arrange your ideas. You may wish to follow a least-to-most important order of points, for instance, or arrange the divisions of your paper according to some inherent connection in meaning (one main idea leading logically to another). There are many ways to order points, but there should be a *reason* for the sequence you choose. Never order points randomly.

If the outline is to be turned in with the paper, there are considerations of form as well:

1. Begin all items in the outline with capital letters.

2. Make all main points and all subpoints generally parallel in structure. (See Coordination, p. 291.) Note that the main points in the sample outlines above are nouns and the subpoints begin with verbs.

3. If subpoints are stated, never list an A without a B. Incorrect:

   III. Backswing

      A. Keep eyes on ball

4. Do not list sub-subpoints. Save minute details for the paper. Avoid:

   I.

      A.

         1.

            a.
            b.

The real test of a good outline is whether or not it produces a well-organized paper. For this reason, many teachers do not require students to turn in outlines with their papers. Whether an outline—at least a mental one—has been followed will be obvious from how well—or how poorly—a paper is organized. Some teachers, however, consider the planning stage to be so important that they require outlines with papers in order to encourage students to complete this part of the writing process.

Whether a formal outline is required or not, you will write better papers if you follow a plan. Whether writing a theme for Freshman English, an essay examination for another course, a speech, or a business report, you will find an outline to be not only an aid to better communication but a timesaver as well.

ORGANIZATION

Professional writers disagree on how a good piece of writing evolves. Some claim that they don't know what they want to say until they've said it, while others formulate detailed plans before beginning to write. Nevertheless, practically all writers agree on the necessity of shaping their material before presenting it to a reading audience.

Regardless of the approach you use in getting started, you must organize the content of your essay into some logical sequence of thought before completing the final draft. (See Outlining, p. 7.) As Strunk and White say, "Writing, to be effective, must follow closely the thoughts of the writer, but not necessarily in the order in which those thoughts occur" (*Elements of Style*, p. 10). Logical organization is as important as clear language in communicating your thoughts.

There are many ways to organize an essay, but the simplest and clearest is to state the main idea of the paper in a concise opening paragraph, then write a separate paragraph for each major division of thought, and end with a short concluding paragraph which brings the paper to a satisfying close.

The *introductory paragraph* is the foundation of an essay. It should begin with a lead which engages the reader's interest; then comes a succinct statement of the paper's main idea. (See Thesis Statements, p. 364.) You may also wish to suggest in the opening paragraph how the paper will be organized, but never do this by listing your main points. If a reference to organization is desired, it should be combined with the thesis statement, as in this example:

Everyone can't be a Jack Nicklaus, a Nancy

Lopez, or even a George Archer, but if you're

spending your Sundays on the golf course, you
may as well try to be. If you're a novice
golfer, you know that driving can be
especially embarrassing because there are
usually people watching you struggle off that
first tee. [These first two sentences are the
lead.] By following five simple steps
[organization indicator], however, you can
soon end this period of uneasiness and send
the ball down the fairway just like the pros
[thesis].

The importance of a paper's opening paragraph can't
be overemphasized. In addition to arousing the reader's
interest and stating what the paper will do, it may also
suggest how the paper will be organized and even, as in
the example above, identify an intended audience (the inexperienced golfer). In short, the introductory paragraph
sets up the rest of the paper.

After the introduction comes the *body*. The body is the
main content of a paper and therefore should be its longest
part. It must fulfill the promise you have made to your
reader in the opening paragraph. Theme-length papers
should have a paragraph in the body for each main point;
you may use more if necessary. Because the body is the
meat of an essay, the paragraphs which comprise it must
be detailed and fully developed. Catchy beginnings and
endings won't save a paper that's weak in the middle.

A good *concluding paragraph* is the writing equivalent of a graceful exit. One proven method of getting off the stage is simply to sum up the point you have made in the paper, but don't be too obvious about it. Good writers don't end papers with "In conclusion" or "To sum up" for the same reason they don't begin them with "In this paper, I will discuss" or "The purpose of this paper is." Such self-conscious expressions call attention to the machinery of writing and detract from the writing itself.

Instead of concluding an essay on how to drive a golf ball with something so mechanized and dull as "I have explained the five steps in driving a golf ball. These five steps are . . .," you might end with a lighter touch, reminding your audience that the process involves five steps (readers can look back over the paper if they want to review them) and that if a person wants to be a good golfer, they're worth remembering:

> In sports, good habits can be learned almost as easily as bad ones. This is certainly true of driving a golf ball. It may seem awkward at first, but if you'll follow these five simple steps, you'll soon master the first stage of the game. Who knows? Maybe you <u>can</u> be the next Jack Nicklaus or Nancy Lopez.

A paper's concluding paragraph is important because it is the last impression left in the reader's mind. It can produce a sense of finality or a sense of incompleteness.

One more thing: *titles.* Don't underrate their importance. A title not only indicates the subject of a paper, but it also can serve as an attention-getting device. The title is the first thing a reader sees, and it can get an essay off to a slow start or a fast one. "Golf," for instance, would be a poor title for a paper on how to drive a golf ball because it is much too broad. "How to Drive a Golf Ball" is accurate, but dull. "Getting Teed Off" is a better title because it suggests the subject of the paper and also shows a bit of imagination. "Drive Carefully" is another possibility. If you've entertained the reader, you'll be forgiven for the momentary ambiguity caused by such titles. Titles need not always be witty, but they shouldn't follow a formula. Even "Driving Tips" beats the predictable "How to Drive a Golf Ball."

There you have the components of an essay: title, introduction, body, conclusion. I saved titles till last because many writers do. They find that writing the paper helps them to think of a good one. By the way, long titles went out with the eighteenth century.

After you have written a first draft, examine its parts to see how they have taken shape. The way an essay looks on the page gives you some idea of whether it is well-structured. As a general rule, introductions and conclusions should be the shortest paragraphs in the paper; the paragraphs making up the body should be considerably longer and fully developed. Any other pattern usually means trouble.

TONE AND AUDIENCE

Tone is the writer's attitude toward the subject; audience is the writer's reading public. Expository writers adjust their tone to fit their audience. Especially when writing about inflammatory issues or subjects about which you have very strong feelings, you may have to compromise between your attitude and a tone which will effectively reach your reading audience. Suppose you are outraged by welfare laws. In writing on the subject, you must "tone down" your anger in order to convey to your readers the impression that you are treating the subject intelligently and not just emotionally. Tone, then, reflects attitude toward the subject modified by attitude toward the audience.

There are as many writing tones as there are human attitudes, ranging from the lightly humorous to the gravely serious. In writing, as in speaking, *how* something is said is as much a part of meaning as what is said. While a speaker has the aid of voice inflections, facial expressions, and gestures to communicate attitude, a writer must rely on word choice alone. (See Diction, p. 299.) Consider the difference between these two sentences: "My father is an alcoholic" and "My old man's a drunk." The two statements convey exactly the same information, but they are worlds apart in tone. The first implies sympathy, or at least an unwillingness to pass judgment, while the second conveys an attitude close to contempt. A writer must be aware of the quite different impressions two such statements would make on a reader.

At some time during the process of composition—at the latest before writing the final draft—you must decide on the attitude you wish to convey. Once you have determined a tone, you must be consistent. Switching from light to serious treatment, for instance, would only confuse your reader. In proofreading, if you detect a word or expression which doesn't fit your attitude or your audience, a thesaurus (dictionary of synonyms) may help you find a more suitable term, or you may wish to restate the idea completely.

In general, most of the papers you write in college should be relatively serious in tone. Do not, however, confuse a serious tone with a dull one. There is room for imagination in *any* kind of paper. A serious tone simply means one which suggests that you are treating your subject with respect. Except in papers which are clearly humorous or satirical, this is the tone you should strive for.

In deciding on tone, which is reflected by word choice, the writer must keep the reader ever in mind. Consider the different tones—and language—you would use in letters describing a college experience to your best friend, your parents, and your ex-high school principal. Similarly, in writing papers you must match tone to audience and express yourself in terms which the general reading public is likely to understand and to consider appropriate. With this principle in mind, you should avoid the extremes of language. Don't use pretentious words and specialized terms which most of your readers may not be familiar with; at the other extreme, avoid expressions which the average person is likely to consider in bad taste. Admittedly, there is some guesswork involved in writing for this "average" adult reader, but the level of language in a good daily newspaper is a fairly reliable guide.

In a college writing course, there may be the temptation to write for the teacher instead of a wide reading audience. This is a mistake. Sometimes it results in mediocre, inane essays devoid of imagination; sometimes it results in overwritten papers with the big words and pretentious statements which some students mistakenly assume most English teachers like.

A more productive approach is to write for a general college reading audience—your classmates and other students, your teacher and other professors. One way to look at this is to write essays which you would be proud to have published in your campus newspaper. Keeping such an audience in mind should help you strike the right balance in selecting clear, standard, yet interesting and expressive language.

PROOFREADING AND EDITING

A well-organized paper on an interesting topic will still be an inferior piece of writing if it is filled with errors in mechanics, grammar, and style. Such errors simply sabotage anything you might have to say in a paper. To guard against them, you must carefully proofread and make corrections before putting your papers into final form.

Most writers find proofreading and editing to be the most tedious part of the writing process, but those who neglect this crucial last step will later regret it. Good writing is difficult to achieve, and writers either pay the price in time and effort during writing, or they pay it later in the form of irritated readers, low grades, or, in the case of professionals, rejection slips. Publishers, in fact, won't even read a carelessly written submission. A final manuscript must be as clean and as error-free as you can make it. To do less is a disservice to yourself and an insult to your readers.

Before putting a paper into its final form, go over it carefully at least twice. Read your paper the first time for flow of thought. Make sure that each sentence leads smoothly into the next and that the relationship between the paragraphs is clear and logical. Add, relocate, or omit sentences to improve unity. (See Paragraph Unity, p. 328.) Supply transitions wherever needed. (See Transition, p. 372.)

Then read the paper a second time, concentrating on each individual sentence. Check for good sentence structure, accurate word choice, and correct grammar, punctuation, and spelling. Use the Proofreading and Revision Guide at the beginning of the book, and consult the Handbook on points about which you are unsure. Make corrections immediately. Don't trust your memory. If you're a poor speller, read the paper again, but read it backwards this time so that you'll be sure to concentrate on spelling alone.

Now you are ready to put your paper into its final, polished form. Recopy or type carefully, incorporating all the corrections noted on the previous draft. Don't waste your earlier efforts by hurried or careless final copying. Now put your paper aside for a while. Later, proofread it one last time and neatly make any necessary final corrections.

Productive proofreading and editing take time, but it is usually during this final step of the writing process that the greatest improvements are made. More important, it is by thoughtful proofreading and editing that you learn the most about writing. If you carefully correct each paper, you will eventually find yourself mentally editing out errors as you write. Then you will be on your way to becoming a writer.

Much of the aversion toward writing can be eliminated if you have a method or a plan, such as the one outlined in this chapter. Getting started is almost always the hardest part, but writers can't wait for inspiration. Most of the writing we do, whether in school or in the professional, business, or social world, is done to serve a practical purpose. Rarely do we have unlimited time in which to complete this writing. Writing papers for an English class is realistic preparation for the other writing you will be doing throughout your life. The skills you learn by writing

essays—clear expression of thought, a sense of organization, correctness of form—will help you communicate
better in any type of writing.

With practice and experience, writing will come easier,
but it will never come easy. Professional authors agree on
one thing: Good writing is more a matter of perspiration
than inspiration. But when you've said what you have to
say as well as it can be said, the sweat is worth it.

2

Types of Essays

The types of essays discussed and exemplified in this chapter represent common ways of thinking and communicating in writing. The process paper, in which the writer gives instructions on how to do something, is one of the most practical and most popular kinds of writing. Classification helps us organize a mass of data into manageable categories, and we make comparisons every time we have to decide between alternatives. Analysis enables us to break down a subject into its parts for close examination, and we engage in argument whenever we try to persuade someone to agree with us. It is human nature to describe interesting people, places, and things and to relate the significant or amusing events of our lives. The character sketch, description, and narrative papers reflect these common modes of communication.

Each section in this chapter defines a particular type of paper and gives advice on what to do—and what not to do—when writing it. The lists of sample topics indicate the kinds of subjects appropriate to each type of paper; the sample essays illustrate the organization of each kind of paper. These essays should be used as form models only, and you may be required to write either a longer or shorter paper than the examples. Regardless of length, however, the organizational principles remain the same. Each type of paper requires a certain format, which is explained and illustrated in the section.

This chapter may be used in either of two ways. If you are assigned a specific type of paper, you may study the appropriate section beforehand to see what is required in the way of organization and subject matter. If you are permitted to write an essay of any type, you may begin your paper and then study the appropriate section once you have decided which form best fits your preliminary draft. Then you should revise your paper according to the guidelines of the section. (For a writing plan, see Types of Writing Assignments, p. 3.)

Organization is an important part of writing, but it is only one part. To be a good writer, you must master a variety of skills. This chapter will enable you to meet the form requirements of an assigned paper or to find the form best suited to what you want to say. Establishing the format of your paper early in the writing process frees you to concentrate on expressing your ideas as effectively and as accurately as possible. Good organization will not guarantee a good paper, but you can't have a good one without it.

PROCESS

A process paper tells someone how to do something. As simple as this may sound, many people find it hard to give instructions. Have you ever been unable to assemble something because of unclear instructions or been hopelessly confused by someone's directions on how to get to a certain place?

The main problem with giving instructions is that the person who already knows how to do something often assumes too much on the part of the beginner. As a result, the teacher may confuse the learner by omitting necessary steps, by failing to organize the process into an easy-to-follow form, or by using terms unfamiliar to the beginner.

The best way to avoid these problems is to put yourself in the learner's place. The final test of the clarity of your instructions is not whether *you* can follow them, but whether a beginner can. Ask yourself what you would need to know and the order in which you would need to know it if you were just starting to learn the process. Then answer these questions in your instructions. State your directions in language the average person can understand, being especially careful to define technical terms. At points where a beginner is likely to go wrong, warn against common mistakes. Write your instructions as if the learner were actually present and carrying out the process. Use the instructional (technically, the imperative) voice: Don't write "A golfer should keep the left arm straight," but "Keep your left arm straight." Address your learner directly.

Above all, you must *plan* your paper. Planning is an indispensable part of any writing assignment. If the plan is solid, the essay is likely to be a success. If the plan is illogical, no amount of verbal heroics will rescue the paper. Many writers devote as much time to planning a paper as they do to composing it. (See Outlining, p. 7.)

The first step in planning is choosing a suitable topic.

Select a process you can do well. Don't attempt to teach someone how to ski, for instance, if you are just starting to learn. It's all the better if your process is an unusual one. Yet even if you have not mastered an extraordinary skill, topics as common as how to apply makeup or how to change a flat tire can make solid, useful papers. If you begin with a broad topic, limit it to a specific skill that you can teach in the space of a theme. If, for example, you choose to write about golf, don't attempt to tell someone how to play golf in one short paper. Instead, narrow this subject to one phase of golf: driving, chipping, or putting.

After selecting and limiting your topic, the next task is to organize the details of the process in the order in which you wish to present them. The "how-to" theme is one of the easiest to organize because a process follows a chronological, or time, order. Organizing this type of paper, then, is simply a matter of determining the major steps of the process, deciding on all the substeps, and then listing these steps in the order in which they must be done. Once you have identified and ordered these basic steps, you have the main divisions of your paper. If you choose to write on a process which requires the use of materials (including tools), you may be able to work the needed items into your introductory paragraph. If the list is extensive, "Gathering materials" could be the first step of your process.

Some writers like to establish a tentative plan (called a preliminary outline) before beginning to write. Others prefer to formulate a plan after the first draft is written and then reorganize the paper to fit the plan. This second approach is especially useful if you're having trouble getting started. Whether your writing plan precedes the first draft or evolves from it, you must not omit this important organizing step.

Sample Essay

Thesis: Learning to drive a golf ball
requires the mastery of five steps. [Note that
the outline thesis statement may be worded
differently when it is worked into an
introductory paragraph.]

  I. Stance
 II. Grip
III. Backswing
 IV. Downswing
  V. Follow-through

                 Getting Teed Off

    Everyone can't be a Jack Nicklaus, a Nancy
Lopez, or even a George Archer, but if you're
spending your Sundays on the golf course, you
may as well try to be. If you're a novice
golfer, you know that driving can be especially embarrassing because there are

usually people watching you struggle off that first tee. By following five simple steps, however, you can soon end this period of uneasiness and send the ball down the fairway just like the pros.

The first step in learning to drive a golf ball is to master the proper stance. Above all, your stance should be comfortable. After teeing up the ball, determine the place of your stance by allowing the clubhead to rest flat on the ground parallel to the ball and just behind it. Keep the middle, or "sweet" part, of your driver head centered on the ball. Now stand where you can naturally grip the club without cocking the clubhead off the ground or getting it out of parallel with the ball. Next, spread your feet apart at a distance approximately equal to the width of your shoulders. Keep your feet parallel and flat on the ground, toes pointed straight ahead and weight equally distributed on both feet. Bend your knees slightly and bend slightly toward the ball at the waist.

Once you have assumed a comfortable, balanced stance, make certain that you have the correct grip. There are several types of grip, but the interlocking grip is the most popular. In positioning your stance, you have already gripped the club at the end. Now place your left thumb parallel upon the end of the grip (the leather or rubber on the end of the club). Holding this position, wrap the fingers of your left hand around the grip, keeping the hand firm but relaxed. Now place the shank of your right thumb over your left thumb, keeping both parallel to the club grip. Next, interlock your left forefinger with your right little finger, gripping the club slightly tighter with the right hand. Now check to see that the clubhead is still resting flat on the ground, centered on and parallel to the ball. You have now "addressed" the ball (adjusted the club in preparation to hitting it).

The first movement in actually swatting the ball is the backswing. It is essential from this point on that you never remove your eyes from the ball. Slowly bring the clubhead straight back from the ball in a natural arc. Allow your left leg to bend slightly with the turn of your body and the raising of the club. Your right arm will also bend slightly, but you must keep your left arm straight, no matter how unnatural it might seem. Stop your backswing when your hands reach head level. Keep your feet firmly planted, toes pointed straight toward the ball.

Upon completing the arc of your backswing, begin your downswing without hesitating. The downswing is the backswing arc in reverse. Bring the clubhead straight toward the ball, smoothly increasing club speed and being careful to keep the left arm straight and the wrists stiff. During the course of the downswing, allow your left-hand grip to tighten naturally. Attain power and speed by exerting the right arm. At the moment of impact, both arms will be pointed straight down the club's shaft and body weight will be shifting forward. If all has gone well, you will hear a rewarding "thok" as the clubhead solidly strikes the ball.

The follow-through is simply the completion of the natural body movement of the downswing. Push the clubhead "through" the ball, snapping, or "breaking," your wrists at the point of impact for power and leverage. Maintain club speed after impact and lean slightly forward. Avoid the temptation to look up immediately to see where the ball is going. Instead, keep your head down and your eyes on the spot where the ball was teed, until you have completed the follow-through. Allow your body to turn

slightly to the left, pivoting on your right
foot. Continue the arc until the club is
resting slightly above your left shoulder.
Now you may look up at your ball coming to
rest two hundred yards down the middle of the
fairway.

In sports, good habits can be learned
almost as easily as bad ones. This is
certainly true of driving a golf ball. It may
seem awkward at first, but if you'll follow
these five simple steps you will soon master
the first stage of the game. Who knows? Maybe
you <u>can</u> be the next Jack Nicklaus or Nancy
Lopez.

Sample Topics

Possible topics for a process paper are limited only by
the number of activities you can do well. You must be
careful, however, not to write your paper on a topic that
resembles a process but really isn't one, such as "How to
Make Friends." Also avoid trivial topics, such as "How to
Ride an Elevator." While your process should be serious
and useful, it need not be commonplace. An extraordinary

skill you have mastered or an unusual job you have done involving a process could make interesting papers.

Any activity involving a series of sequential steps which you can do—and which someone else may be interested in learning— is an acceptable topic. The following list suggests some possibilities:

Waterskiing

Making a dress

Surfing

Decorating with decoupage

Building a campfire

Decorating your room

Bagging groceries

Making wine

Executing the double somersault

Silk-screening

Catching a pass

Making pickles

Spelunking

Antiquing furniture

Fielding a grounder

Doing the butterfly stroke

Building a stereo system

Changing oil

Building a terrarium

Rolling a strike

Wood carving

Building a windmill

Making a lamp (or other useful object)

Cutting firewood

Canoeing

Baking homemade bread

Serving in tennis

Transplanting a tree

Working a fast-food counter

Pitching a tent

Making a foul shot

Insulating your home

Making jelly

Plucking a chicken

Deep-sea diving

Checking out groceries

Fly-fishing

Skateboarding

Painting your room

Blocking downfield

Stopping a leaky faucet	Constructing a solar-heating system
Constructing a mobile	
Tuning a guitar	Making a dress

Note: Avoid cooking topics which involve essentially giving a recipe.

CLASSIFICATION

Classification enables a writer to impose order on a mass of details by grouping them according to shared characteristics. The act of classifying is a natural one. All of us have heard such common remarks as "War novels and detective stories are all right, but I really love historical romances." When you write a classification paper, you simply do in a deliberate and formal manner what you often do in a less conscious way: organize a mass of data into manageable categories. You may think of classification as a "types of" paper, and it may be on people or things.

Most people possess some unique traits, but classification ignores individual differences and stresses characteristics shared by certain types. This is stereotyping, a premise which both the reader and the writer of a classification paper must accept. Stereotyping can be informative and even entertaining, but it can also be misused. Especially when writing about people, you must take special pains to make your stereotyping reasonable and fair. Your classification should reflect your own point of view, but it must not be prejudiced or quirkish. For instance, papers on "Black and White Students" or "Men and Women Drivers" would be poor classifications because the types have at least as many similarities as differences and therefore don't constitute valid, distinctly different types. Furthermore, such topics are sure to offend a large number of readers. In addition to intelligent selection of types, the details you use to identify each type must be so reasonable and credible that a reader cannot legitimately question them as traits typical of the group. In short, your types, whether people or things, must not only be intelligently conceived but immediately recognizable by the characteristics you attribute to them.

A classification identifies shared traits *within* each type, but it does not deal in similarities *between* types. While the types you identify must be parts of the same general subject, they must be distinctly different from one another. A paper on "Three Types of Movies: War, Detective, and Mystery" would not work because the detective and the mystery categories overlap. Comparisons may be mentioned in transition between paragraphs, but you must break down your subject into types which can be discussed as separate, self-contained units, such as "War, Detective, and Western Movies."

Since two-category topics such as "Country and Folk Music" and "The Public Servant and the Self-Serving Politician" lend themselves best to *comparison* essays, you should select a subject which can be broken down into more than two parts for your classification paper. Three categories seem to fit a theme-length paper well, but there is no magic number. Completeness is an aim only of highly formal, scientific classification, so you can afford to be selective. The categories of war, detective, and western obviously do not account for all types of movies, but it would be unrealistic to try to cover them all in one essay. Instead of attempting to cover your subject completely, select a few interesting major categories, keeping the desired length of the paper in mind.

The categories you choose should, of course, be revealing. "Three Types of High School Teachers: Math, Biology, and History" would not make a worthwhile paper because the standard of classification is merely the subject matter taught. Classifying teachers according to personality, classroom manner, teaching approach, or a combination of these would make a better paper. And be sure to avoid trite classifications, such as "Good, Bad, and Average Teachers."

Another important consideration in selecting categories is balance and parallelism. Your types must fit together logically. "Three Types of College Women: The Playgirl, the Bookworm, and the Geology Major" is not a balanced division of parts because the first two types are categorized according to their dominant character trait and the third is categorized according to major. "The Playgirl, the Bookworm, and the Goody-Goody" is a more balanced plan. To enhance balance and organization, discuss parallel features of each type whenever possible. You could, for instance, describe the appearance, classroom behavior, study habits, and social life of each type of college woman.

When appropriate, use distinguishing labels to identify your types. This advice applies especially to light papers on types of people. Either Bookworm or Brain, for instance, is more colorful than "the serious student." But remember: If you label one type, you must label them all. Be sure to make labels parallel in form and capitalize them throughout the paper. To avoid repetition, you should vary label names with synonyms. Facetious labels should never be used in a serious paper.

Sample Essay

Thesis: Football games can bring out the

abnormality in usually ordinary people, as a

look at three types of fans will show.

   I. The Expert

  II. The Drunk

 III. The Socialite

Football Fanatics

Fall and football season always bring an assortment of weirdos out of the woodwork. The word "fan" is short for "fanatic," and a look at three prominent types of spectator will show how accurate that word is.

Every stadium row has at least one self—proclaimed Expert. Ever since he played second—string guard on the junior varsity, he's been an avid football fan. A veritable storehouse of useless statistics and pigskin trivia, he can even tell you how the first—string quarterback did on his biology mid—term. So devoted is he to the sport that he always carries a transistor to the game

with him. He wants to stay right on top of
other games and get their scores before
anyone else in the stadium. When he hears an
interesting score, he is more than happy to
loudly report it to those around him. If
you're lucky and happen to be seated next to
this guy, you'll get free instruction on all
the finer points of the game. You may still be
trying to figure out which is the home team,
but he'll be giving you all the inside
information on blitzing linebackers and
flip-flopping coverage. This fan is a lot
like the guy-next-door--if you live next door
to Howard Cosell.

While the Expert is mostly a harmless
bore, the Drunk is physically dangerous. He
seems to go out of his way to batter innocent
people about the head and shoulders and give
them bourbon showers. The only time he gets
quiet is when he pours himself another drink.
He may have fallen over six people to get to

his seat, but he still assumes the fetal position to sneakily pour a drink. At such times, the Drunk likes to think of himself as a sly rogue, pulling wool over the eyes of all the "straights" around him. By the second half, however, he has thrown caution to the wind and is blindly cheering for the wrong side, cursing the referees, and trying not to be sick. He is especially pleasant to sit near if you've brought your young daughter or your best girl from down on the farm to the game.

While the Expert considers the football stadium his private pressbox and the Drunk mistakes it for a bar, to the Socialite a football stadium is a combination showcase—bedroom. He comes to games mainly because they are good places to be seen and to see others. He's much more interested in spotting his friends and seeing who their dates are than he is in watching the game. In fact, the Socialite doesn't know a field goal from a first down, and he periodically yells "hold that line" while his team has the ball. Since his main interest is creating an impression, his first choice of a date is the Big Woman on Campus type. If that fails, he will settle for the sexpot. He gets no pleasure from these dates except for the envy he imagines they create in others. As the Socialite loosens up, he sometimes waxes amorous. He and his date celebrate touchdowns with a kiss. The Socialite has even been known to celebrate a five-yard penalty with a kiss. Having no genuine interest in the game, he quickly becomes bored and fills the empty hours with frequent trips to the concession stand, the john, anywhere he might win friends and influence people. Back at his seat, his specialty is yelling at an acquaintance ten rows down while the rest of the stadium is quiet. He especially likes cheers with curse words in them because they make him feel sophisticated and naughty. The Socialite's section of the stadium should be X-rated.

Fortunately, these specimens of abnormal psychology are common only to Saturday afternoons in the fall. At other times of the year, they revert to the drab, ordinary creatures they really are. But just thinking about them has inspired me to make a decision: I think I'll stay home and watch the game on TV this Saturday.

Sample Topics

In selecting a topic, keep the introductory pointers in mind—especially the necessity of selecting a subject which you can break down into at least three separate but parallel types. Remember that your types should be recognizable and credible, but they need not be obvious. No one wants to read a paper on "Three Types of Eating Utensils: Knives, Forks, and Spoons"! A classification paper may be either light or serious, and it may be on either people or things. For instance, you may write on such topics as types of

High school teachers	Musicians
College professors	Movie stars
People in your dorm	Sports announcers

Girls you have dated	Politicians
Boys you have dated	Political activists
Studiers	Parents
Churchgoers	Ministers
Rock fans	Drinkers
Salespeople	Vacations
Comic strips	Careers
TV commercials	Grading systems
(or shows)	Philosophies of education
Movies	Economic systems
Books	Political systems
Weddings	Life-styles
Funerals	Colleges
Music	Poetry (or other art forms)

COMPARISON

Comparison, sometimes redundantly called "comparison and contrast," is a statement of similarities and differences. Obviously, in writing a comparison paper, you would discuss contrasts as well as likenesses.

In the course of everyday life, we constantly make comparisons in deciding between such alternatives as eating out or at home, taking a summer job or going to summer school, or buying a flashy sports car or a practical sedan. In making such decisions, most people weigh the advantages and disadvantages of the alternatives. Like all the other common types of papers, a comparison essay is simply a formal version of a natural thought process.

A written comparison, however, differs from a mental

one in the number of choices you may consider. You may begin the mental process of selecting a car by considering three or more alternatives, such as a sports car, a compact, or a sedan. But in writing a comparison paper, you must narrow your choices to *two*. Comparing three or more things in a paper is like trying to juggle too many balls. The usual result is poor organization and a confused reader. Even in making mental comparisons, we often reduce our choices from several to two which can be closely examined.

Once you have narrowed the alternatives to two, the next task is to organize the comparison. Consider the important features held in common by the two things you are comparing. In selecting a car, the points of comparison could be economy, performance, and styling. This gives you the main points of your paper; within each division you can examine similarities and differences, advantages and disadvantages. In determining these points of comparison, you must be selective. For a theme-length paper, choose three to five features which most people would consider important.

Finding the most important features held in common by the two things you are comparing is the best way to organize a comparison essay. Do not use the so-called opposing or divided pattern of organization permitted by some writing handbooks—an approach which allows the writer to lump together all the information on one item and then all the information on the other. This method is easy, but it does not constitute true comparison. The writer using this divided pattern merely supplies blocks of information and leaves it to the reader to do the actual comparing. But readers won't do this much work for a writer. This fact leads us to what is perhaps the most important principle of expository writing: *Don't expect your reader to do any of the mental work for you.* Applied to the comparison essay, this means simply that *you* do a point-by-point comparison. Don't provide the raw materials and expect your reader to do it for you.

Sample Essay

Thesis: <u>Close Encounters of the Third Kind</u> is a basically realistic, serious movie, while <u>Star Wars</u> is a delightful space fairy tale.

   I. Setting

  II. Character

III. Message

Earthly Desires, Divine Fulfillment:

<u>Close Encounters</u> vs. <u>Star Wars</u>

  <u>Star Wars</u> and <u>Close Encounters of the Third Kind</u> both crashed upon the seventies movie scene like meteors. Their phenomenal box—office success bears witness that the films have captured the imagination of the viewing public. Film critics have treated both movies reverently, extolling their

symbolism and mythic implications. The two films are alike, however, in only superficial ways. Close Encounters is a basically realistic, serious movie, while Star Wars is a delightful space fairy tale.

The most obvious difference between the two films is their settings. The action of Close Encounters never leaves the earth. Its big scenes take place in rural and suburban Indiana and at Devil's Tower, a mountain in Wyoming which differs from the ordinary only in the flat top necessary for the alien-landing. The locales in Star Wars, on the other hand, provide a visual treat, mixing bone-lonely, ravaged landscapes with breathtaking views of strange planets and starry expanses as seen from a spaceship. Star Wars is set in the exotic future, Close Encounters in the dreary present. Close Encounters offers the promise of the wide-open spaces and change of scenery that

earthlings desire from time to time; <u>Star</u>
<u>Wars</u> fulfills that promise.

    <u>Star</u> <u>Wars</u> also treats the viewer to a more
varied and interesting cast of characters
than <u>Close</u> <u>Encounters</u>. Both movies are
populated by humans and strange space
creatures, but here the similarity ends. The
people in <u>Close</u> <u>Encounters</u> are all quite
ordinary. The main character, who works for a
power company, and his wife and children
constitute a typical middle-class American
family. The computer-age scientists look and
talk like computer-age scientists, and even
the art-dabbling, back-to-the-land single
parent of the child who is spirited away by
the aliens is something of a cliché. Only
slightly more interesting are the aliens
themselves, with their spindly bodies and
oversized heads, which the audience must
strain to glimpse through the haze
surrounding their spaceship.

By contrast, <u>Star</u> <u>Wars</u> gives us an irreverent space-age pirate (Han Solo), a young Sir Galahad (Luke Skywalker), a kindly but strong father figure (Obi-Wan Kenobi), and even a lovely damsel in distress (Princess Leia). The bad guys counter with the insect-faced Stormtroopers and that blackest of villains, Darth Vader. In addition to these assorted humans and humanoids, <u>Star</u> <u>Wars</u> has introduced new figures into American pop culture in the form of the lovable R2-D2 and the quarrelsome but cute Wookie. Even the minor characters are unforgettable--ranging from the hooded, slave-trading dwarfs to the futuristic mutants in the comic-masterpiece bar scene, where the humans and not the mutants seem to be the freaks.

Consistent with these differences in locale and character is the fact that the message of <u>Close</u> <u>Encounters</u> is much more serious than any ideas in <u>Star</u> <u>Wars</u>. <u>Star</u> <u>Wars</u>, in fact, really may not say anything at all, in spite of all that has been attributed to "The Force." Toward the end, the movie does touch on some ideas concerning the inadequacy of science in a real pinch. When all seems lost, Luke Skywalker heeds the word of "The Force," turns off his computerized targeting device, and blasts the evil Death Star to kingdom come just by trusting the inner voice of his instincts. It is, of course, also possible to see the movie as proof that good triumphs over evil in the end, but haven't faithful moviegoers always known (or hoped) that to be the case? If <u>Star</u> <u>Wars</u> has a message at all, it is either slight or trite.

Again, <u>Close</u> <u>Encounters</u> is another matter. Simply because the locales and the characters are so ordinary, the movie says more about real life. The hero, if he can be called that, is as earthbound and as

powerless as the knocked—out power company he
works for. His life is a dull, stifling
routine, a point driven home by the
dispirited family squabble over dinner and by
the amazed stares of his fellow suburbanites
as he wrecks his yard to build his dream model
of Devil's Tower. The audience observes a man
who is as ordinary as the station wagon
his wife leaves him in, a beleagured
middle—class American who needs a close
encounter of <u>any</u> kind. His desire for a change
spurs him to chuck job, family, and home in
pursuit of the dream symbolized by the
fleeting image of the magic mountain xeroxed
on his brain. When our hero boards the
spaceship at the end of the movie, he doesn't
know what awaits him, but he seems confident
that it's better than what he's leaving
behind. The point of the movie is that life on
earth has become so colorless that the only
hope of happiness lies in a completely new and

different kind of existence, promised by the benignly smiling visitors from a presumably better world.

Star Wars makes us forget our troubles by rocketing us into a colorful, lively world of the future. Close Encounters reminds us of how dull earthly life can be, but offers hope of change to anyone bored enough to seek it, no doubt making the film appealing to those who like their escapism tempered by reality. But moviegoers who prefer old-fashioned entertainment decked out in the latest style find that seeing Star Wars once is not enough.

Sample Topics

Remember to limit your topic to two things which are sufficiently alike to warrant comparison, yet different enough to make comparison revealing and interesting. The following list suggests only a few of the items which lend themselves to worthwhile comparison:

Fifties rock and seventies rock

Traditional and progressive education

College student attitudes of the sixties and the seventies

Two political systems

The liberated and the old-fashioned woman

The founding fathers and modern politicans

Buddhism and Christianity

Baptist and Episcopalian

Fundamentalists and Charismatics

Time and *Newsweek*

Playboy and *Esquire*

TV programming then and now

The old-time vs. the modern baseball hero

Wartime and postwar Viet Nam

Two literary figures

Foreign policy now and then (at any previous period)

Country and folk music

The Beatles and Kiss

Art films and porno movies

Traditional and contemporary sexual mores

Traditional and counter-culture weddings

Democrat and Republican

Two novels or books

TM and Est

MS and *Ladies' Home Journal*

Playboy and *Cosmopolitan*

Hollywood: The Golden Age and today

The old and the new China

Pop country vs. pure country

Traditional and avant-garde poetry

You may wish to compare two well-known personalities who have something in common. For example,

Billy Graham and Oral Roberts

Walton and Jabbar

Gloria Steinem and Phyllis Schlafly

Warren Beatty and Burt Reynolds

Carter and Kennedy

Brown and Reagan

Reggie Jackson and
Pete Rose

Jane Fonda and Raquel
Welch

Hugh Hefner and Helen
Gurley Brown

John Denver and Mick
Jagger

ANALYSIS

Analysis means breaking down a subject into its main components so that these parts may be closely examined. In addition to being the major method of studying literature (see Writing about Literature, p. 195), analysis is used in solving everyday problems. If a lamp doesn't work, you may attempt to find out why by first checking into the simple possibilities that the bulb is burnt out, the cord isn't plugged in, or the electricity is off, then moving on to more complicated analysis of the condition of the cord and receptacle, and finally to the lamp itself (which would require dismantling it and examining its parts). Similarly, before taking an apartment, you would do well to analyze its main features, such as expense, location, space, and privacy.

Superficially, analysis resembles each of the previous three types of papers—classification, comparison, and process—but in each case there is an important difference. Like classification, analysis involves dividing a subject into parts, but while classification selects from a broad subject several categories for discussion (such as three types of recreational vehicles: dune buggies, vans, and campers), analysis examines the major features of a narrower subject (such as the economy, performance, and styling of the Volkswagen Rabbit). Although economy, performance, and styling could also be used as the major points of a comparison essay, a comparison would entail examining *two* cars under each heading, whereas an analysis must be limited to one. An analysis even resembles a process paper, but again there is an important difference. While a process describes how to do something (for instance, how to tune a car), an analysis may describe how something *works* (the car's engine, for example). In planning your analysis paper, keep these distinctions in mind.

Analysis, then, is the close examination of the major parts of a narrow subject. You may be able to adequately analyze the combustion engine in a theme, but you could not hope to cover a broader topic such as "How Cars Work." Even in writing on a sufficiently limited subject, you must be selective in the items you choose to analyze. An analysis must cover all the major parts of your subject, but not necessarily every detail. A paper analyzing the economy, performance, and types of bolts used in a particular car would present an odd selection of components. Balance is a related consideration. The components you designate for analysis must be relatively equal in importance. The use of selectivity and balance means that you would eliminate types of bolts from an analysis of a car and replace it with a more significant feature such as styling.

While you must eliminate features of lesser importance, you must be careful not to omit any major ones. An analysis of a politician, for instance, would not be complete without some discussion of voting record. Because a theme-length analysis must be reasonably complete within a short space, you should choose a subject which can be adequately covered in three or four major points.

Sample Essay

Thesis: The student radicals of the sixties were motivated by three factors.

I. Dislike of discipline

II. Adults' inflated opinion of youth

III. Genuine idealism

Student Rebellion in the Sixties

The adage that people rarely are moved to action by a single motive is probably well-founded. A case in point is the troubled last half of the 1960s. The majority of rebellious students on American college and university campuses were not inspired by a single motive but by a mixture of three factors.

The least flattering of these three motives was an aversion to discipline. Campus radicals equated middle-class mores and life-style, lumped together under the label of establishment values, with dull and meaningless routine. The orderly, comfortable life that many older Americans had worked for years to achieve was viewed as a rut. Traditional academic structures, such as required courses, tests, and grades, came to be regarded as meaningless customs. Books such as <u>The Greening of America</u> forecast a new consciousness characterized by permissiveness and impulsiveness rather than by disciplined structure. Middle-class sexual standards were openly flaunted by disciples of the New Morality. "Shacking up," once considered shameful, became the accepted thing. Loafing was considered "cool," and stealing was romanticized as "ripping off" a corrupt society.

Many students, despairing of ever changing the traditional structure of higher education, sought a freer life-style in counterculture systems such as communes. Many of those who remained on the campus to fight the battle tried, often by violent means, to convert the university into something resembling a commune. Many of these campus

radicals masked, possibly even to themselves,
under the guise of idealism an egotistical
contempt for authority and an unwillingness
to accept the fact that often the price of
achieving a worthwhile goal is self—sacrifice
and hard work.

The older generation should not be too
quick to condemn these campus radicals,
however, because it is partly to blame for
their disruptive behavior. Many student
radicals were motivated, at least in part, by
the gaudy predictions so—called responsible
and influential adults were making about the
younger generation of the sixties. "You're
the most worldly—wise, best—educated
generation ever," the news media blared,
until many young people began to believe it.
This was nothing more than a cop—out, a
cynical passing—of—the—buck. "We've fouled
up the world," these breast—beating adults
said. "We've given you Viet Nam, racial

strife, and crooked politics," they said,
"but _you_, brilliant and idealistic youth, are
going to get us out of this mess."

Youth worship was most blatant in college
classrooms, where it became fashionable for
professors to dress and talk like their
students and to affect a new humility. "I'm
going to learn more from you than you will
from me," many of them announced. Meandering
"rap sessions," sprinkled with the language
of the street, replaced lectures and
structured discussion. Grades were inflated;
a _C_ became a cause for shame and irritation.
Once—secure teaching jobs hung by the thread
of student evaluations. Many of those who
refused to play the new game were replaced by
willing younger professors. Administrators
installed campus radicals in important
decision—making positions and protected
student lawbreakers from laws enforced
outside college walls. Spiro Agnew's famous

attack upon educators as "effete intellectual snobs" rang true for much of the public.

Thrust into the seat of power, many campus radicals must have had mixed feelings about their success in winning responsibilities with which they were in no way prepared to cope. The destructiveness of the drug culture and the failure of such radical-supported innovations as Pass/Fail, open admissions, racial separatism on campus, and student-run colleges in general seem to indicate that the assessment of the rebels' leadership abilities was overly optimistic.

This is not to say that the radical movement was utterly negative. Mixed in with the less noble motives of the campus radicals was a measure of sincere desire to improve the quality of education, campus life, and American life in general. While in some campus radicals idealism was negligible or nonexistent, in others it was the prime

motive. The radicals primarily motivated by
genuine idealism listened to the other side
and even compromised when necessary. They
sometimes participated in sit-ins and
strikes, but they did not trash buildings,
lock out administrators, or stone policemen
(although they sometimes "stoned" themselves). While many college administrators and public officials cowered
before the threat of violence, it was this
quality of genuine idealism that clear-
thinking citizens respected. Without
it, the counterculture movement on campus
would have been a total loss.

These student radicals did have an impact
on campus values. Mainly because of their
influence, college students and professors
now dress and wear their hair (or beards) the
way they please. The sixties' cry for
relevance has left a legacy of valid new
courses, such as environmental studies, and

more learning-by-doing, both on and off
campus. Students don't run the universities
of today, but they do play a bigger role in
decision-making than ever before. The
distance between professor and student has
not been eliminated altogether--and probably
shouldn't be--but a more humane relationship
has evolved as the result of the "role
leveling" of the sixties. We have reaped
these and other benefits from a social
movement which was neither as irresponsible
as its detractors contend nor as noble as its
supporters would have us believe.

Sample Topics

Because analysis requires breaking down a subject, the
topic you choose must be divisible into at least two parts.
In general, you should avoid highly technical subjects,
such as nuclear reactors and Old English verse forms,
which would appeal mainly to specialists. You may, however, analyze a fairly complicated subject of general interest, such as how an electric car or solar heating system
works—if you can discuss the subject in terms the average
reader can understand. You may use simple drawings to
help clarify such analyses, but illustrations should be tied

in with your writing and should not be so numerous as to dominate the paper.

You must know your topic especially well because an analysis explains the "inner workings" of a subject. Don't write on a technical subject unless you can explain it simply and clearly. The following topics could make good analysis papers, depending upon your personal knowledge of the subjects. If you can't find a suitable topic in the list, maybe it will help you think of your own. Analyze:

Common advertising techniques (or TV commercials or magazine ads)

The appeal of a popular comic strip ("Doonesbury," "Dick Tracy")

The formula of a type of TV show (talk shows, situation comedies, soap operas), or of a currently popular type of show, or of one particular show

The formula of a type of movie (car movies, disaster movies, porno movies, Bogart, Woody Allen, Ingmar Bergman, Charles Bronson movies)

The formula of a type of book (self-help, historical romance)

The outstanding features of a type of music (rock, jazz) or of the music associated with a particular person or group (Scott Joplin, Janis Joplin, Barry Manilow, the Beatles, the Rolling Stones)

The philosophy of a type of magazine (such as men's adventure or liberated woman) or of a particular magazine (*Time, Cosmopolitan, Esquire*)

The appeal or performing style of a popular entertainer (musician, comic, actor)

The dynamics of a cultural ritual (beauty contests, rock concerts, the Academy Awards)

The main features and assumptions of a custom (dating, weddings, funerals)

The reasons why something is changing (why Congress is getting more power, why the public is becoming dis-illusioned with politicians, why more controls are being placed on the press)

The causes of a political phenomenon (why we got in-volved in Viet Nam, why we lost the war, why the Arabs and Israelis can't agree, how Carter got elected, why _____ should be our next president)

The causes of an economic phenomenon (inflation, reces-sion, unemployment, high energy costs, high housing costs, tight credit)

The causes of a social phenomenon (women's liberation, high divorce rate, "living together")

Why something is or isn't working (crime control, the postal system, racial integration, Congress, the method of electing a president)

The main doctrines or common attitudes of a particular group or sect (political, religious, social, philosophical)

The philosophy behind an educational convention (required courses, exams, grades, a particular grading system)

Why a problem exists (why college graduates are having trouble getting jobs, why teenage pregnancy is increas-ing, why college students go home on weekends)

The causes or main issues of a current controversy on your campus

Student attitudes or values as reflected by popular slang
   expressions

Student attitudes toward a controversial issue (perhaps involving a random survey or student interviews)

ARGUMENT

Unlike process, classification, comparison, and
analysis, argument is not so much a way to organize a
paper as it is an attitude on the part of the writer. An
argument, in fact, may be structured as an analysis—for
example, in a paper examining a political hopeful's personal and leadership qualities in order to support the candidate's election. An argument also may take the form of a
comparison—for instance, in an essay supporting one
political candidate over another by comparing the two.

Argument is so distinctive in tone and intent, however, that it deserves its own category. In the four types of
papers covered in the previous units, the writer is explaining or describing something and is not attempting to *persuade* the audience to think a certain way. This is the distinctive quality of argument: It is heavily slanted in an attempt to persuade the reader to agree with the writer. The
writer of an argument paper may use explanation or description, but the primary purpose of an argument is to
convince.

The writer of other types of papers assumes that the
reading audience is neutral. The writer must interest this
audience, but not necessarily persuade it to think a certain
way. In contrast, the writer of an argument paper assumes
that the audience is not neutral but in opposition. Put simply, argument papers are not directed at those who may
agree, but at those who do disagree. After all, the readers
who already agree don't need to be convinced. It is this

premise of an audience which must be persuaded that gives the argument paper its special qualities.

In an argument paper, therefore, your point of view must be especially definite and strong. Wishy-washiness is bad in any type of writing, but in an argument it is disastrous. You must leave no doubt as to which side of an issue you are on. Every detail of the paper must be directed toward supporting *your* way of thinking. If you mention opposing arguments, do so only to discredit them. Never write a "There you have both sides—take your choice" paper for an argument.

Instead, clearly and firmly state as your paper's thesis the premise of your argument and then support it vigorously. This support may take the form of sound reasoning and examples, or it may be buttressed by formal evidence such as research and statistics. If researched information is used, be sure to give proper credit. (See Chapter 3, especially Plagiarism, p. 332.) If you use statistics, keep them simple and interpret them for the average reader by explaining how they support your argument. If researched information and statistics are incorporated, don't allow them to dominate your paper. As in all other types of writing, most of the content should be your own.

In making a strong case, watch out for emotionalism and overstatement, especially sweeping generalizations. To make your argument logically sound, you must qualify general statements such as "American women are oppressed" in order to make them reasonable: "*Many* (or some or most) American women are oppressed." (There are at least a few liberated ones!) Moreover, you must avoid irrational statements which reflect your own emotionalism and appeal to the prejudices of your readers—such as "I hate the press for hounding Nixon out of office. Reporters think they're better than the rest of us."

Argument attempts to persuade others to adopt a particular point of view by showing that point of view to be the most logical and intelligent one. This aim should be achieved by sound reasoning and facts, not by emotional, opinionated statements.

Sample Essay

Thesis: Required general education should not be eliminated from the college and university curriculum.

   I. Adds to high school learning

  II. Provides needed review

 III. Allows time to adjust

  IV. Broadens education

Don't Junk Basic Studies

A college degree is no longer the meal ticket it once was, which is probably the main reason that more criticism is being directed at higher education in America then ever before. Colleges and universities across the nation are evaluating their programs with the stated intent of making higher education more practical and more relevant. From the point of view of many students, the least relevant and least useful component of their college education is the segment of courses variously labeled as core courses, basic studies, or general education. This set of courses typically includes instruction in composition, humanities, history, and social and physical sciences. In most American colleges and universities, students complete courses in all these subjects, usually during their first two years of college, before officially selecting a major. Many students feel that these first two years could be better spent taking courses in their majors. I believe, however, that this segment of courses from various areas of learning serves a useful purpose and should not be eliminated from the college and university curriculum.

A main argument of opponents of basic
education is that it is a repetition of high
school courses. Valid college–level basic
studies courses, however, explore subjects
in greater depth and on a more mature in–
tellectual level than their high school
counterparts. For example, the college
history professor, usually less restricted by
outside pressures than the high school
teacher, may present a more accurate view of,
say, America's treatment of the Indians or
the role of blacks in American history. In
addition, teachers and textbooks scarcely can
keep up with new scientific discoveries and
the rapidly changing social, economic, and
political scene, so these courses need not be
mere repetition of high school material. In
these areas, college basic studies courses
often give students an up–to–date version of
material studied in high school.

In addition, there is something to be said

for these courses even if they do repeat high
school material. All but the college students
who were fortunate enough to attend excellent
high schools can benefit from review. The
fact that a student has been previously
exposed to material does not mean that it has
been learned. Falling SAT scores in English
and math seem to bear this out. Furthermore,
most colleges and universities provide
testing procedures by which those students
with exceptional aptitude or superior high
school preparation may be exempted from
college courses involving material which they
have already mastered. Most of today's
entering college students, however, can
benefit from more work in basic studies.
Virtually every college freshman has had some
form of high school English, for example, but
some have never written an essay, and many of
those who have written essays have not had the

benefit of careful marking by their overworked high school English teachers. In other words, many college freshmen have had no practice in writing or have had practice which has not helped them correct their writing problems. Considering the wide range of motivation and abilities and the overload of students and extracurricular duties which the high school teacher has to contend with, it is likely that what is true of high school English is also true of other subjects as well. Therefore, until public education in America is upgraded, college basic studies courses are needed to compensate for inadequacies in high school education.

Another reason for not eliminating basic studies from the college curriculum is that these courses allow the beginning college student a period of time for adjustment. Most college freshmen are just out of high school and living on their own for the first time. Taking courses to which they have had some prior exposure eases the shock of transition from high school to college and gives the new college student time to adapt both socially and academically. Furthermore, many students come to college because of parental pressure or because they have been told that they need a college degree in order to survive in a competitive world. Many of these students have only the dimmest notion of what they want to major in. A sampling of various courses can help them locate their interest and aptitude.

Yet another justification for basic studies courses is that they broaden a person's education. Americans are notorious for valuing something according to how useful it is in a material sense. Nothing is more frustrating to an English teacher than the student who complains, "I'm going to be a computer programmer. What good will literature ever be to me?" The science teacher probably experiences the same frustration when the humanities student questions the need to study physical science. This all-too-common attitude is based upon the assumption that the only function of higher education is to teach a marketable skill. The great educator John Henry Newman, in The Idea of a University, remarks that "Since cultivation of mind is surely worth seeking for its own sake. . .there is a Knowledge which is desirable, though nothing come of it, as being of itself a treasure, and a sufficient remuneration of years of labor." What Newman is saying is that learning is worthwhile in itself, whether you can buy a hamburger with it or not. General education supports this commendable philosophy.

Admittedly, what is being taught in basic

studies courses in most colleges and universities probably should be taught in high school. But it is futile to discuss what should be done in American high schools as long as teachers are burdened by so many nonteaching duties and by an overload of students of widely divergent ability and motivation. It is unlikely that these problems in public education will be remedied in the near future. In the meantime, basic studies courses might be accelerated so that students could complete them during the first year of college, and students could be given a wider choice of basic studies courses, but this important component of higher education should not be eliminated at the present time.

Sample Topics

Choose a subject which is likely to interest a general reading audience. Arguing, for instance, that your hobby is fun or that your parents are unfair would be of mainly personal interest. Furthermore, a writer is apt to treat highly personal subjects too emotionally. Write on a topic about which you feel strongly but can also argue intelligently and rationally. In general, an argument will be more appealing if it is on an issue of current national or local (including campus) interest. Check a recent newspaper or newsmagazine for such topics.

Since argument requires the use of a body of information to persuade the audience, select a topic on which you are well informed. You may increase your knowledge with additional reading, but don't turn your essay into a formal research paper unless that is part of the assignment. Here are a few suggestions for topics which may be of current interest. You could argue:

In favor of a change you would like to see in the educational, political, or social system

A social issue (whether the New Morality is good or bad, whether the press has too much freedom, whether movies should be censored, whether integration is working)

For or against a university requirement or custom (required classes, class attendance, the grading system, coed dorms, sororities and fraternities, homecoming, cheerleading, intercollegiate sports, athletic scholarships)

For or against a popular custom or institution (marriage, organized religion, political campaigns, the electoral college, income taxes)

For or against a popular form of entertainment (car racing, rock concerts, X-rated movies, TV game shows)

For or against any currently controversial issue on campus or in national politics

Against a recent newspaper editorial or letter to the editor

CHARACTER SKETCH

A character sketch is potentially one of the most interesting types of essay. It is human nature to be intrigued by people—especially unusual people. Newspapers and magazines are filled with sketches of such individuals, as are our letters and conversations. The purpose of a character sketch is to bring its subject to life—to capture in a short space the essential nature of a person. The character sketch paints a portrait with words.

A portrait has a better chance of being appealing if its subject is interesting to begin with, so write your character sketch on a unique, colorful person you have known. But don't attempt to tell everything you know about this person. Shape your sketch around several key traits which will make your character memorable to the reader. As in most theme-length papers, three or four main points should suffice. The nature of the person you are characterizing, of course, will determine what these points are. Traits of lesser significance and even interesting details which don't fit the dominant characteristics you select should be omitted. The essential personality of your subject is the thesis, or controlling idea, of a character sketch.

In developing the features of your character, it is of the utmost importance that you be specific. If you say that a person is funny, give some examples that will make your readers laugh. If the character's appearance is significant, describe it in detail. (If it isn't, don't include it.) In addition to examples and description, two other common characterizing devices are dialogue and anecdotes, or brief stories illustrating specific traits. *Brief* is a key word. Don't turn your sketch into a story. (See Narration, p. 96.)

A character sketch resembles an analysis. In both types of essay, a subject is broken down into several important components. A sketch, however, should not be written in the style of formal analysis. For instance, you should not write anything so stiff as "The first point of Mabel's character is fastidiousness." For a character sketch, "Mabel's a dedicated fussbudget" will do nicely.

The character sketch gives you the opportunity to be especially imaginative and creative in style. It should be fun to write, as well as fun to read.

Sample Essays

Thesis: Housekeepers are often stereotyped, but ours was truly unique.

   I. Appearance

  II. Work Habits

 III. Hypochondria

  IV. Fussiness

Mighty Minnie

Kim Dickens (Student)

I don't remember exactly when Minnie started working for my family——just that it was some time during my first years of school. She was far from being the typical housekeeper. In fact, I don't know of any stereotype Minnie would have fit. She was an original.

Minnie was very good about getting to work on time—when she felt like it, that is. We could spot her a mile away by her combination traveling and work uniform. She always wore a faded blue turban (which she proudly swore was its true color), a black, knee-length dress, a freshly starched purple apron, and what I called her "Mary Poppins shoes." Over her right arm she carried a bulky pocketbook, which she had been planning to get rid of for weeks, and a flowered umbrella to ward off unfriendly dogs—or maybe unfriendly people. She marched up the drive as if she were leading an army into battle.

It made no difference to Minnie if my sisters and I were still asleep when she arrived. She would simply start her work in the kitchen. The amount of noise she could create by clanging pots and pans together or slamming cabinet doors was astounding. I suspected she did it on purpose to get us out of bed, or at least to wake us up, although day after day, she apologized for being so loud and clumsy. I always suspected that her "Hope ah dint 'sturb ya'll's beauty naps" was not totally sincere.

When we finally dragged ourselves to the breakfast table, she would greet us with a big smile and a hearty "How's ya'll dis mawnin'?" My sisters and I would mutter a sleepy "Fine" and then out of politeness ask how she was. Before we could get away, Minnie had told us exactly how she was. Poor woman, she probably held the world's record for the amount of suffering endured by one person. If her blood pressure wasn't too high, it was too low. She always had a terrible cold which was about to turn into the flu, or possibly pneumonia, her back was aching, her legs were tired, the

arthritis in her hands was "flaring up"
again, and, to top it off, her head was "jus'
'bout to bus' open."

Despite her "poor health," Minnie somehow
was still able to find enough energy to fuss
at us for not straightening up our bedrooms.
Often she would threaten us with "I gonna tell
yaw daddy" or "I'm jus' gonna leave dis mess
here to letchaw mama see it when she git
home." Minnie's threats were successful until
we finally discovered her weakness—snuff. We
soon learned that we could talk her into
cleaning up almost anything for us if we would
walk to the store and buy her some snuff. For
the remaining years that she worked for my
family, my sisters and I were always able to
use that strategy on her.

It has been several years since Minnie got
too old to work. She still comes by
occasionally to see how we're getting along
without her and to reminisce about when we

were younger. And each time before leaving, she shakes her head and says with a note of pride, "Ah allus knowed ya'lls gonna turn out awright!" Then she marches down the drive as if she were leading an army into battle.

Thesis: Virgil, a man I once worked with, was full of contradictions.
   I.   Uneducated, but smart
  II.   Unsophisticated, but witty
III.   Good-natured, but bad-tempered

Virge

    I wanted to spend the last summer before entering college in my hometown, but when I couldn't find a job, I set out for Virginia Beach in search of employment and excitement. I didn't find much excitement, but I did land a job on a construction crew. That's how I met

Virge, one of the most unforgettable people I've ever known.

Virge may have been ignorant, but he was far from dumb. He couldn't read the fractions on his measuring tape, but that didn't stop him from being a skilled carpenter. "Three marks past the eight," he would measure, and it always seemed to come out right. Virgil not only had trouble with fractions, but also with his own age. He didn't know how old he was. One day he told me he was "either thirty-four or thirty-five." Then he added, "The last time I had to know how old I was was when I got married, and it got me in trouble that time." Virge thought he was still married, but he wasn't sure about that either. Although Virge could barely read, not only did he possess a driver's license and a car, but he had a nice apartment near the beach and was living year-round in an area where rich people come for vacations. Not bad for a backwoods Kentuckian with a third—grade education.

Virge also got a lot of fun out of life. He was constantly breaking me up with his Gomer Pyle wit. "People come here to the beach from north, south, east, and other places," he once said. Then he waited for me to give him the look that such an oddball remark deserved. On one particularly rough day, Virgil, up to his knees in mud under a house, said, "You know, carpenters have almost as much fun as people." Virgil's humor was almost always directed at himself. One morning he came to work looking very depressed. When I asked him what was wrong, he replied, "I'll never trust television no more. They said Brylcreem would git girls. Well, I put it all over my head and walked around town half the night, and not a damn one follered me!" On another occasion, when Virge was about to leave for Kentucky on his vacation, we asked him which route he was going to take. "Well, I can't drive into the ocean," Virgil reasoned, "so I already know the direction. I figger if I start drivin', I'll git there." In a week, Virge was back to work right on time. He said he'd found Kentucky and that it was located "somewheres close to Tennessee."

I considered Virgil such a good-natured person that I was really surprised to find that he had a mean streak. Maybe it really wasn't meanness, but backwoods pride. Anyway, an incident occurred while we were working together that I'll never forget. It was always in the 90s, and one blistering morning Virge reported to work wearing a black leather jacket. The jacket was especially puzzling because Virge was very proud of his tan and never even wore a shirt, but we were working on separate crews that day and I didn't get a chance to ask him about it. Later that afternoon when we were riding home from work, I learned the purpose of the jacket. "It's a good thang the foreman didn't git on my back today," Virge said angrily. Then he pulled up the jacket and showed me the .38 caliber revolver stuck in his belt. From that day on, I was always anxious to see what Virge was wearing when he picked me up for work.

I think I was the only one on the crew who really liked Virge. Not only did he give me a ride to and from work for a mere two dollars a week, but on my last day he called me aside and said, "I don't care what they say about college boys, you're all right." It's a compliment I'm proud of because Virge didn't think much of education or of the people who'd had "their brains warfed" by it. If he hasn't shot the foreman, I suppose Virge is still doing OK. Anyway, I hope he is. I don't care what they say about illiterate hillbillies. Virge was all right.

Sample Topics

Write your sketch on an interesting, unique person whom you know well, but avoid such potentially sentimental and clichéd topics as "My Father," "My Sweetheart," and "My Little Sister" unless you can take a fresh approach to these subjects. Remember that you must make your character as memorable to a stranger (your reader) as he or she is to you.

Also avoid subjects which are likely to bore the average reader, such as "perfect" people or inspirational types ("My High School Coach")—again unless you can treat them freshly (satirically, for instance). You might write your sketch on such topics as these:

The most unforgettable person you've ever met

A person you wish you'd never met

The most ridiculous (phoney, humorous, weird, unpredictable) person you've ever met

Any person who differs from the norm and is truly what we call a "character"

DESCRIPTION

As a character sketch attempts to bring a person to life with words, a description attempts to bring a place or thing to life. Although a character sketch deals with a person and a description deals with places or objects, both strive to capture the essential nature of their subjects. Therefore, many of the writing principles pertaining to the character sketch also apply to descriptive writing.

The controlling idea of a descriptive essay should be the special quality of the subject you are describing. Figuratively speaking, you may think of this quality as the "personality" of your inanimate subject. Since the success of a descriptive theme depends upon your making your subject vivid to the reader, it is obviously to your advantage if you choose a topic with inherent interest. This does not mean, however, that the subject of a description must be exotic. In fact, capturing the special quality of something ordinarily taken for granted can make an excellent description paper. After all, this is what a good painter does with a bowl of fruit. Such subjects as a duplicate brick ranch in suburbia or the typical doctor's antiseptic waiting room could make interesting descriptions.

As the dominant personality of the subject of a character sketch determines selectivity, the special nature of the place or thing you are describing dictates what details to include and what to omit. Do not include any details, however interesting, which do not develop the central idea of the description. Remember that you are not so much describing your subject in its entirety as you are communicating its essential quality. The details you do select should fit together to create a dominant impression (such as the commonness of a brick ranch home or the cold sterility of a waiting room), usually presented in a spatial order.

The most important principle of descriptive writing is "Show, don't tell." Don't merely discuss the dominant impression of your subject—make the reader *see* and *feel* it. Figurative comparisons (metaphors and similes) are one means of achieving this aim. For instance, "The abandoned farmhouse was very sad" neither paints a picture nor communicates sadness. The writer asks for a response, but doesn't evoke one. In contrast, "The abandoned farmhouse, *with windows like forlorn eyes*, stood hopelessly awaiting its family's return from the fields" creates a visual image and is also more likely to evoke a sense of sadness.

In using figurative language, be sure that the emotional associations fit the effect you desire. Suppose you had compared the curtainless windows of an abandoned farmhouse to starry eyes. Not only is that image difficult to visualize but, because of the generally positive feelings associated with starry eyes, it also works against the impression of sadness. And watch out for mixed metaphors. "The windows of the dilapidated farmhouse, like forlorn eyes, reached out their arms for the family which had abandoned it" is a mixed metaphor—eyes don't have arms. In addition to mixed metaphors, avoid any figure of speech which has been worn out by overuse, such as "winter wonderland" and "hard as a rock."

One last word of caution about figurative comparisons: Use them when they are appropriate, but don't overdo it. A metaphor or simile in every sentence, or even in several consecutive sentences, is too much of a good thing. Do, however, be specific in every sentence. Remember that in a description you are painting a picture for your reader. General words such as "vegetation" or even "trees" don't make a reader *see*. Word pictures such as "a grove of gnarled oaks" or "a sprinkling of spindly pines" do.

Sample Essays

Thesis: My favorite hill was almost like a

playmate to me.

  I. The hill in summer

II. The hill in winter

My Hill

Marty Begin (Student)

There was a hill behind our sprawling ranch house back in the good old days when we lived out West: a treeless, eroded, sage-covered hill. The slope below our house was the beginning of what was called Nine-Mile Hill, so-named not because it really was a nine-mile hill, but because truck drivers dreaded it like the very devil and thought that a hill which could ruin a good diesel deserved its very own name. Nine-Mile Hill began the ascent from the basin of the Rio Grande Valley to the desert plateaus west of Albuquerque. Our house was at the top of the first rise, and it was this hill below our house that we children loved so much.

In the summertime, we used to make stick horses out of old broom handles and race our mounts down to the bottom of the hill, hurdling the sagebrush, taking shortcuts through the arroyos, and ending our derby with a swim in the muddy irrigation ditch which lay at the foot of the hill. Sometimes we would startle a wild rabbit, which would bounce away in fear of being trampled by our sturdy chargers' hooves, and the chase would be on. At night, when it was too dangerous to gallop up and down the rough incline, we would stable our mounts and play kick-the-can. The hill was good for this because the sagebrush, arroyos, and deserted gopher holes made excellent hiding places. We would play this game until it was impossible to see the can in the dark anymore, or until our mothers ganged up and came with switches to haul us home. But we never abandoned our favorite playground for long. About halfway down the hill, there was an old ruin, the remains of an adobe hut.

There wasn't much left of it except some fallen logs and two eroded walls, all of which was nearly covered with sand. We never tired of excavating it; broken bits of rust—red pottery and Indian arrowheads were scattered throughout the surrounding ground, and it was always exciting to dig up such valuable finds. The old ruin was our clubhouse, our Fort Apache, our camping ground, and our animal cemetery. We had a passionate and possessive love for this, our private, all—purpose place.

I don't think we ever loved our hill so much as in the wintertime, though, when snow covered it. That was about the only time the hill actually <u>looked</u> pretty. The snow coated the uneven bare ground and the straggly, twisted sagebrush clumps with a magic blanket, making it look like a fairyland of miniature mountains, valleys, and forests.

But smothered under woolen underwear, sweaters, jackets, knitted mittens, fuzzy earmuffs, and two pairs of pants, we would gaze only briefly at this wonderland. We were more interested in its usefulness than its beauty. With our feet and bottoms we would plow a path down its face, winding around mountains and forests, through and over valleys. After trampling the snow firmly with boots and smoothing it with frozen mittens, we would line up our sleds, cardboard boxes, and garbage can lids, and then take turns sliding down. We played a rough game, and many a time the sissies went home with snow in their collars and tears in their eyes. After a couple of hours, the one who had completed the trip the most times without a mishap would be proclaimed winner. He would then be allowed to divide the rest of us into two teams. His team would take to the protection of the snowcapped ruin, and the two armies would

battle it out in the Snow Fight of the Year.
This battle usually ended in bitter words,
tears, and frozen anatomies, all of which
were forgotten by the next day. All through
the winter, we molested our hill like this;
only school or extremely bad weather or
mothers or some other catastrophe could keep
us from our playground.

Time changed our hill. The old ruin was
demolished by man-made monsters, and a
subdivision replaced our ski slope. We kids
have all grown up since then and gone our
separate ways, but the weedy, eroded,
sometimes snow-covered hill remains the same
in my memories. Time won't change that.

Thesis: The cabin was primitive but cozy, a
refuge in the storm.
   I. Interior construction
  II. Furnishings
III. Effect of snow

Hunters' Retreat

David Tolley (Student)

The cabin was silent except for the muted sound of the wind outside. The venison and biscuits had been eaten and praised, and the hunters had settled themselves in a loose semicircle about the hearth. Several hours had been filled with sips of bourbon and talk of the hunt. Now, at midnight, only the cigars remained. The men drew closer to the dying fire, heavy wool blankets draped about their shoulders. Thoughts replaced conversation.

The cabin was not a modernized copy, but the real thing. Its rough logs, now grayed with age, had obviously been hewn by hand. Instead of mortar, the cracks between the logs were filled with clay mixed with straw to hold it together. Tiny bits of straw protruded from the chinks like an old man's whiskers. At regular intervals, large squared rafters lodged firmly into the walls to form a cathedral ceiling. The heavy oak door stood exactly centered at the front of its arch. The floor too was made of tightly pegged, heavy oak boards, now worn smooth by many boots. The cabin's only concession to modern comfort was its two glass-paned windows, which apparently had never been cleaned.

The furnishings were almost as primitive as the construction. A walnut gunrack stood to the left of the blackened stone fireplace. The guns had been cleaned and oiled. They stood like sentinels in the rack, whose bark hadn't even been stripped away. In a back corner was a rickety cot which no one used, preferring instead the sleeping bags scattered about the floor. Exactly in the center of the cabin sat a round maple table awaiting the next meal or poker game. The table was decorated by a huge oil lamp and surrounded by orange crates turned on end. Around the walls, heads of deer and several smaller game hung at random. Battered cooking utensils, tools, and assorted sacks dangled from iron pegs driven between the stones of the fireplace. A large bearskin rug lay before the fire where the men stretched their feet.

The coziness of the tiny fortress only made the hunters more mindful of the snow, which lay cobwebbed in the corners of the two bare windows. Periodically, an angry gust of wind would boom the cobwebs away, and new ones would begin to form. Moonlight reflected off the white surface outside through the glass and competed with the light from the dying embers for the darkest corners of the one-room cabin. Wavering columns of smoke rose from the hunters' cigars to form a thick gray-blue screen which all but obscured the massive oak beams. When not gusting, the wind kept up a steady moan down the chimney.

Although the fire had not been replenished

since it cooked the deersteak dinner, none of
the men moved to thrust another log on the
coals. They preferred instead to sit quietly
and enjoy the security of the cabin and the
companionship, each man with himself, of
this moment.

Sample Topics

Practically any place or thing can serve as the subject
of a description, but it must be a place or thing with a
dominant quality that you have identified and can focus
your description upon. Selecting a subject which has
evoked a strong response in you will give your paper a
better chance of success. But you must comprehend your
own response before you can recreate it for your reader.

In general, avoid broad subjects such as "New York
City" or "The Rockies" unless you can capture the *essence*
of such places in the short space of a theme. Don't write a
travelogue. Problems of specificity and selectivity will be
lessened if you choose a narrow subject. For example:

Your room

A friend's room

Your favorite place

Your ideal home

Your high school hangout

Main street in your
 hometown

Your grandmother's attic

Your most prized
 possession

Your favorite childhood
 possession

A special gift you've
 received

An object you associate
 with a special person

Your first car

Your white elephant

An auction barn

A country church

A city cathedral

A bait and tackle shop

A riverbank at dusk

The surf during a storm

The Northeast woods

A locker room

A laundromat

A beauty shop

A classroom

A billiard hall

A country store

The city after dark

A Southern town square

The beach at dawn

A thunderstorm

A scene after a heavy snow

Spring or fall in the mountains

The Maine coast

A dentist's office

A tavern

A barber shop

A dormitory lounge

A funeral parlor

A dance hall

NARRATION

A narrative is, quite simply, a story. As a description attempts to capture the sense of a place or thing and a character sketch the nature of a person, narration attempts to capture the spirit of an event. The narrative writer communicates an experience to the reader—or, as Hemingway said, "how it was."

Also like a character sketch and a description, a narrative must show and not tell. Try to make your reader experience the action as it unfolds. To do this, you must make your narrative detailed and specific. A story obviously cannot exist without description and characterization, but the emphasis of narration is upon action. As the great storyteller Flannery O'Connor said, if nothing happens, you don't have a story. A narrative, then, answers the question "What happened?" The best ones, in addition, communicate what it felt like.

Obviously, it helps if you have a good story to tell, but the *way* a narrative is told is as important as the story itself. Some storytellers can make a mediocre story interesting; others can make a good story dull. The difference often lies in what writers call *pacing*. A good narrator keeps things moving along. You can achieve brisk pacing in your narrative by eliminating all irrelevant or fringe details and by reducing the action to its essence. Don't include anything that doesn't advance the story line. Digressions distract and irritate, and subplots have no place in a brief narrative. Nor should you insert blocks of characterization and description. Characterization, especially in a short narrative, is implied by what the people do, so it takes care of itself. Description also will take care of itself if you describe the action in concrete terms. Thus, both characterization and description will be present in their proper proportions if you just concentrate on vividly recounting the action.

Good pacing also means that your narrative should build to some sort of high point—a climax. The reader's interest should steadily increase as the story develops (as the plot thickens) and then peak at the climax, where the narrative comes to a head.

Narratives obviously differ from formal essays. Whether you're writing a funny story meant merely to entertain or a serious narrative designed to illustrate a point, your controlling idea should never be stated in a formal thesis sentence. Use the opening of your paper to get your story rolling. Never tell in advance what the narrative is supposed to do. Narratives don't discuss—they illustrate. The "point" of a funny story will be clear if your reader is entertained. The way the story is told must carry this point. You can't say "You had to be there." You must *put* your reader there.

Similarly, the point of a serious narrative must be clearly implied by what happens and the way it is told. Modern writers can't take the easy way out by stating at the end of a narrative "The moral of this story is. . . ." If a story has a moral, or theme, it should not have to be stated: It should be *illustrated* by the action. This means, among other things, that you must get off the stage quickly. Some narratives simply end at the point of climax. If you want a concluding paragraph, make it brief. Never use it to sum up the meaning of your paper, as you might do in essays designed explicitly to inform.

There are two other special considerations pertaining to narration. One concerns the sequence of events. Most narrative essays are written in straight chronological, or time, order. (The events are described in the sequence in which they happened.) You may, however, shift back and forth in time, provided that you make such shifts clear to the reader by means of transitional signals (such as "I was reminded of the time when . . ." or "When Janet was just a child, she had . . ."). Avoid lengthy flashbacks, however. They can be distracting.

A second technical consideration is point of view. There are basically two types. A story written from a first-person point of view is told by a narrator involved in the action. The writer employing this point of view uses personal pronouns such as "I," "me," or "we." The other common point of view is third person. The writer using this point of view is not part of the story. This writer describes something that happened to someone else. If you write a narrative from a third-person point of view, you should not refer to yourself in telling the story.

In a narrative essay (as opposed to a short story), the first-person point of view is the more common, especially since you are encouraged to write your narrative on a personal experience. In using first-person point of view, however, you should eliminate as many personal references as you can without creating awkwardness. By necessity, a personal narrative must include many personal references. But if most of your sentences begin with "I," your style will be monotonous.

Because narratives don't really have formal main points, paragraphing is sometimes a problem. In writing a narrative, begin a new paragraph for shifts in action or locale. In dialogue, begin a new paragraph each time the speaker changes.

Sample Essays

Thesis: My greatest thrill was a football game with a storybook ending.

   I. Pregame

  II. First half

III. Halftime

 IV. Second half

   V. The big moment

A Magic Moment

Football season opened Friday night, and
for the first time I had made the team. We
would be playing Richville High, a big
consolidated school in a nearby county.
Although my high school had only six hundred
students, we had always played our best
against this hated rival. Friday's game was
the opener for both schools, but everyone
said the winner would end up conference
champs. Something in the pit of my stomach
told me that one way or another, this game
would be special.

While Coach Wilson was taping my ankles,
he mumbled, "Hope them monsters don't run us
off th' field." When I replied, "I know we're
gonna win," he grinned sheepishly and said,
"I wish I was that sure." My teammates didn't
seem to share my confidence either. They sat
sprawled on the bright green benches, either

silent or talking in subdued tones. After the raucous practices, the quietness seemed strange. Bob Fayette, waiting to get his ankles taped, smirked as if to imply that my remark was just playing up to the coach.

We were battling on the enemy's turf, which put us at a disadvantage to begin with. Not only would they have a big home crowd behind them, they knew the playing field like their own backyard. And then there was their size. Picking a team from a student body of two thousand could turn up some giants, and they looked awesome as they warmed up. In exercise formation, their black and gold dotted nearly half the field. Our traveling squad of thirty—one, fifteen of whom actually played, formed a maroon sprinkle in the opposite end zone. Their smaller players looked as big as our larger ones. The Richville fans had hooted us onto the field.

After the opening kickoff, the

butterflies left my stomach and moved to my legs, where they secreted adrenalin. The crowd, which included virtually every able-bodied citizen of my football-crazed hometown of five thousand, was quickly reduced to a dull background roar. But I could hear the announcer call my name when I made a tackle from my linebacker slot, and my confidence was wildly increased by pride.

Despite our best defensive efforts, we were down 12-0 at halftime, and it could have been worse. It looked like Richville's year. The dressing room smelled of clammy sweat, rubbing alcohol, and impending defeat. As the coach droned defensive adjustments, I felt little ice prickles in my stomach because, against all reason, I still believed the game was ours. The coaches didn't seem to agree. There was no pep talk before the team somberly filed out.

Late in the third quarter, we finally got

a touchdown from our best runner, a little
speedster named Junior Gambell. We also got
the point after, but it looked like it would
end there, 12-7. We chipped away at their
massive front wall for most of the fourth
quarter, but not for steady or long gains
which lead to scores. Our fans had grown
silent, awaiting the end. Theirs were quiet
too, apparently out of boredom.

Then, with just over a minute left in the
game, it happened. Incredibly, the Richville
quarterback, with a five-point lead and the
game running out, dropped back to pass on his
own thirty-yard line. I couldn't believe this
insanity as I drifted to cover the lanky
halfback flaring toward the sideline in front
of me. The quarterback eyed my man, but I had
him covered. Then something whispered to me,
"Let him get open." I instinctively responded
to my mystical coach and laid back. Sure
enough, seeing the receiver suddenly come

open, the quarterback released the ball in
his direction. Just as it reached his
awaiting grasp, I made my move in what I
visualize as a majestic swoop and felt
the sweet leather slap into my hands.
Interception at midfield! Wild cheering
exploded in my ears.

   We huddled in shock and confusion as the
seconds ticked away. Junior cracked the angry
and dispirited opposing line three times in
quick succession, and with seven seconds to
go we found ourselves with our last time-out
on the Richville four-yard line. Time for one
more play. The fans who crossed the mountain
with us had not sat down or stopped screaming
since the interception. I remember barely
hearing the play. "They'll be looking for
Junior again. Don, get ready. Thirty-five, on
two!"

   The rest is like a dream. The quick fake
into the line, the football in my gut, a
head-down plunge through a defender on the

goal line, then the indescribable high, the sheer rush of the end zone.

As it turned out, we didn't win the championship that year. I missed the rest of the season with a blood clot in my leg inflicted that very night. The colors of fall had turned to winter gray when I came out of the hospital with a limp I would carry for a year. But nothing can take that moment from me, nor mar its perfect beauty.

Thesis: Timing and perfect execution made the practical joke work beautifully.

   I. The opportunity

  II. The plan

 III. The execution

A Midsummer Night's Prank

Bill Mabb was the town joke. Nobody, but nobody, believed a word that boy said. He was

always trying to start something. Here he
came, one July night, running up to where a
bunch of us were sitting on the post office
steps, smoking and arguing who was better,
Garvey or Jackson.

At first we ignored him as usual, but he
kept jumping up and down and interrupting.
Finally, Nyoka Canton, a lanky, good-natured
boy and also my best friend, turned away from
the discussion long enough to ask, "What th'
hell you want anyhow, Bill!" Then ol' Bill
tells us the biggest whopper you ever heard.
Says he was out on the golf course messing
around and a big man in a white shirt jumped
out from behind a bush and tried to kill him
with a knife. Nyoka said it was too bad he
didn't. Of course none of us believed a word
of it. Bill had told some about that big
before. But the white shirt made us wonder a
little bit, and anyway Bill wouldn't shut up.
He was wild-eyed and he'd torn his shirt

somewhere, and <u>he</u> seemed to believe his story this time.

The Garvey—Jackson argument had reached its usual standoff and everybody was just milling around cussing and spitting when Little Guinea said, "Let's all go get that guy!" There wasn't much else to do, so everybody agreed it was a good idea. Big Dougie Roth and my little brother went around behind the post office and came back carrying rocks and sticks. Then off they marched, waving their weapons and telling everybody what they'd do when they got him. Bill jumped along behind, whooping and trying to recruit.

Everybody went except me and Bill's brother Becky. Becky said that Bill had just made it up and that he was the "biggest lar in th' world," and I mostly believed him. Of course the others laughed and called us chicken, but we knew they wouldn't be going

either if they really believed somebody was
out there with a big knife. They hadn't any
more than got out of sight past the theater
when Becky got a flash. "Let's you 'n me go
'round the ballpark and beat 'em over there
and scare hell out of 'em." I thought it was a
great idea.

When we got to the bush where Bill said the
man was, we looked around a little bit just in
case Bill had slipped up and told the truth.
Of course he hadn't so we lay down flat on our
bellies in the pitch—black under the bush.
We'd just gotten settled when we heard them
coming, making a lot of noise to prove how
brave they were. Then we saw them in the
clubhouse light. Bill was now in the lead,
pointing the way. The closer they got to the
bush, the quieter they became. I was so
excited that I almost laughed out loud.

About twenty yards from the bush, they
started hanging back. They were bunched

together, creeping forward like a wounded centipede. When the centipede got to the place where the light ended, some of the legs broke off and stayed behind. Little Guinea was pushing his brother Big Guinea along in front of him like a teacart. Nyoka's tall head stood out like a horn. When they got about ten feet from where we were hiding, they stopped dead still and huddled together. It looked like they weren't coming any closer, so ol' Beck and I grabbed the trunk of the bush and shook it like the devil and moaned a little bit for added effect.

The centipede suddenly got its health back and broke into jumping, screaming pieces, led by Bill Mabb. Little Guinea jumped square on Big Guinea's back. Big Guinea wailed "Oh God, he's got me!" and reached over his shoulder and blindly punched his little brother in the face. This caused Little Guinea to fall off, but he forgot to let go of his brother's collar and we heard a shirt rip. Little Guinea was running when he hit the ground. He passed his chubby big brother before he got to the ballpark, retreating the way we'd come. The others no doubt were already regrouping on the post office steps with a new topic of conversation.

After a good fifteen minutes of rolling on the ground and howling, Becky and I casually walked up to the post office and asked them who they thought was better, Garvey or Jackson.

Sample Topics

Write your narrative on an important or amusing incident in your life. The event may be a recent one or a past experience which was meaningful enough to stay in your mind. But in writing about yourself, remember that you are not so much writing *for* yourself as for your audience. You must choose an incident that can be made as significant or as amusing to your readers as it was to you. An objective audience, for instance, may not share someone else's thrill at graduating from high school or receiving a new car. Such topics, unless handled with unusual style, would probably strike a general reading audience as trivial or immature. Also avoid inspirational topics, such as "When I Got Religion." Such experiences may be important, but they are so highly personal that it is next to impossible to communicate their essence. Attempts to do so usually result in clichés and rampant emotionalism. Write on something about which you have strong feelings, but be sure to consider your topic from the reader's point of view. It is also essential that your subject involve action. You can't have a narrative without it. Some suggestions:

Describe an event that was a turning point in your life— something that changed your outlook or philosophy or made you a different person

Describe an intensely emotional personal experience

Describe an amusing incident you observed or were involved in

Write an account of your attempts to deal with a difficult problem or troublesome person

Describe:

Your most embarrassing moment

Your most terrifying moment

Your saddest moment

Your greatest triumph

Your worst defeat

Your most disillusioning experience

3

The Research Paper

Contrary to popular belief, the research paper is not a student-harassment device designed by educators. In fact, teachers will work much harder in preparing you to write the research paper and in grading your finished product than they will on any other type of paper. What, then, is the justification for a writing project which requires so much effort of both student and teacher?

There are several reasons for learning to do research. One is that most of you will be required to write research papers in your other college courses. Those who go on to graduate work will be writing a master's thesis and perhaps a doctoral dissertation, both heavily researched.

There is an even more basic reason for learning to do research. An important part of being educated is knowing how to locate information. The research paper teaches you to use the resources of a library to do just that. You will retain relatively little of the factual information you are exposed to in your college career. Furthermore, your college courses will, by necessity, cover only a small fraction of all the information available even in your major. Knowing how to use a library provides you with a virtually limitless source of information. The research paper is an exercise in locating some of these facts and then working them into an effective piece of communication.

The value of knowing how to do research does not end with your college career. Scholars use research to write books and articles. Teachers on all levels use research to prepare classes. Professional people of all types use research in planning speeches and compiling briefs and reports. In short, learning to do research is one of the most useful skills you will develop in college.

The formal research paper presents a special challenge because it requires, in addition to the demands of good expository writing, that you follow certain conventions special to research writing. Most of these techniques involve incorporating and identifying information taken from books and articles. It is not necessary that you memorize these conventions, but it is absolutely essential that you credit your sources and follow standard models on such matters as footnote and bibliography forms.

Further complicating the process is the fact that the different academic disciplines have different research forms. The various forms, however, have basic similarities. All research writing involves consulting authoritative sources on the subject and identifying, in some manner, the source of wording and ideas other than your own which are used in your paper. Identifying sources serves two purposes: (1) It is a means of crediting others for their work on the subject, and (2) it enables the reader of your paper to retrace the steps of your investigation and read more on the subject from your sources or read a particular quotation or paraphrase in the context of the original source. If you learn to write a research paper by one set of conventions, it should be relatively easy to modify those conventions when you write a paper following a different research form.

A good research paper in many ways resembles a well-written essay. In both types of writing, you must plan the paper and organize its content around a controlling idea or thesis. Some students find a research paper easier to write than an original essay because in a research paper you are allowed (in fact, required) to use the ideas of others for much of the content. The secret of writing a good research paper lies not so much in how many original thoughts you can include as in how well you select ideas from your sources and incorporate them into your paper. Much of research writing is organizing, evaluating, and explaining the ideas of others.

A research paper, however, is not merely the stringing together of quotations and paraphrases from your sources. The reader of your paper will be able to tell whether the information you include has been sifted and under-stood—has passed through your mind and not just your hands—by how you present it. As a general rule, about half the content of a research paper should be quotations and paraphrases and the other half should be your own writing. If you thoroughly research your subject, and *think* while reading, you probably will arrive at some conclusions of your own which are pertinent to your paper. Some of these conclusions may even be in disagreement with the authorities you consult. In any case, approximately half the paper should be comprised of your own original writing.

But what if you cannot offer much original thought on your subject? If you properly handle the information from your sources, you will be doing a lot of writing in prepar-ing your reader for quotations, in incorporating para-phrases, and in explaining, clarifying, and placing researched ideas in the proper context within your paper.

Whether your own information in the paper is composed of original thought or introductory or explanatory material (or, as is usual, a combination), it must be *interwoven* with your researched material. Never present your research in one half of the paper and your own statements in the other. Think of researched information (quotations and paraphrases) and your own comments (introductory, explanatory, original) as two threads which are twisted together to form the total paper.

Most instructors will want to hear your "voice," in one form or another, intermittently throughout the paper. The absence of this writing voice usually is a sign of strung-together, "patchwork quilt" quoting or, worse still, of plagiarism, signified by the professional "voice" of scholars dominating the paper. If research papers are done properly, only the direct quotations will *not* be written in your own writing style. Instructors are very skeptical of dramatic changes in a student's writing style on a research paper. In thoughtful research, the writer peels back the surface layers and gets to the heart of the subject. A research paper involves collecting information, but it requires a *filtering* of that information through your own mind. If researched information passes through your mind on its way into your paper, you will not only have something to add on the subject, but you will say it in your own distinctive way.

TWELVE STEPS TO A RESEARCH PAPER

Step 1: Select a topic.

If you are not assigned a topic or given a list from which to choose, you must select your own. Some possibilities are a subject related to your major, a current issue (in education or politics, for instance), an important social, scientific, or historical event, a literary topic, or a personal interest. Instructors usually require that research writing be done on serious subjects, and your teacher may wish to check your topic before you proceed further.

If you are given a free choice of topic, observe these guidelines:

1. The subject should be something you are interested in.
2. The subject should be potentially interesting to a mature reading audience.
3. The subject should be serious.
4. The subject should be one which your library has information on. (Step 2 explains how you can do a preliminary check on this.)

Step 2: Form a working bibliography.

A working bibliography is a list of books and articles you will use in doing your research and writing your paper. This list should include authors, titles, and call numbers needed to locate each publication in your library. Also write down publication information for both books and articles. If you use these sources in your paper, you will need this information for your footnotes and final bibliography. (For the publication information required, see the sample entries beginning on p. 137.)

There are several guides which you may use in compiling a working bibliography. The most useful is the *card catalog*, which is a file listing all the books in your library. These books are alphabetically arranged on cards by subject, author, and title:

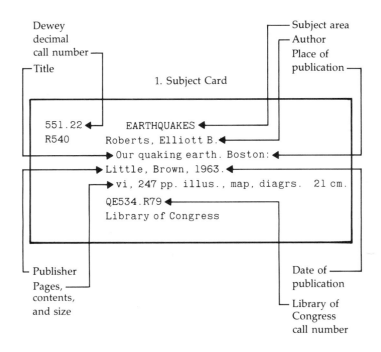

Dewey decimal call number
Title
Subject area
Author
Place of publication

1. Subject Card

551.22
R540
EARTHQUAKES
Roberts, Elliott B.
Our quaking earth. Boston:
Little, Brown, 1963.
vi, 247 pp. illus., map, diagrs. 21 cm.
QE534.R79
Library of Congress

Publisher
Pages, contents, and size
Date of publication
Library of Congress call number

2. Author Card

551.22
R540
Roberts, Elliott B.
   Our quaking earth. Boston:
Little, Brown, 1963.
   vi, 247 pp. illus., map, diagrs. 21 cm.
1. Earthquakes
QE534.R79
Library of Congress

3. Title Card

```
551.22      Our quaking earth.
R540          Roberts, Elliott B. Boston:
            Little, Brown, 1963.
              vi, 247 pp. illus., map, diagrs.   21 cm.
            1. Earthquakes
            QE534.R79
            Library of Congress
```

The card catalog does not include periodicals (magazines and journals) or newspapers. To locate articles of various types, you must refer to special reference sources such as these:

Applied Science and Technology Index

Art Index

Book Review Digest

Business Periodicals Index

Education Index

Music Index

New York Times Index (for newspaper articles)

PMLA Bibliography (for literature and languages)

Readers' Guide to Periodical Literature (for articles in popular magazines)

Social Sciences and Humanities Index (supplemented by separate *Social Science Index* and *Humanities Index* for 1974 to the present)

To use these reference guides, you must understand the code of their abbreviated listings. Here, for instance, is a listing from the *Readers' Guide:*

EARTHQUAKES
  Can we predict earthquakes? J. N. Miller. Pop Sci 163:
  107-111 N'53

  This entry tells you that J. N. Miller's article on earthquakes entitled "Can We Predict Earthquakes?" runs from
page 107 through page 111 in the November, 1953 issue
of *Popular Science Monthly* and is collected in volume 163.
Consult the key at the beginning of the bibliography for the
full title of journals and magazines listed and an explanation of other abbreviations.
  There are several shortcuts you may take in compiling
your working bibliography. Note the publication dates.
Especially on topics of current interest, the more recent a
book or article, the more useful it is likely to be. With some
exceptions, even in researching a scholarly topic you will
find recent books and articles to be the most useful. It is a
good practice to start with up-to-date publications and
work back through earlier ones. You will be able to identify
outstanding earlier books and articles if they are often
mentioned or footnoted in later publications. Try to locate
any source that is frequently cited in your reading. Also
note titles, expecially the titles of articles. The title should
give you some idea of whether an article contains information which will be useful to you.
  There is no standard length for a working bibliography. You will need enough good sources to enable you
to write your paper, but you should use judgment and selectivity to prevent your reading list from becoming un-
manageable. For most papers, you should begin with a
working bibliography of a dozen or so relevant books and
articles, some of which you will discard as you get into
your paper.
  All books listed in the card catalog should be in the
library, but your library may not have all the articles com-

piled in various bibliographies. You must, therefore, check the articles in your working bibliography against the list of your library's periodical holdings; such a list is usually available at the reference desk. This check probably will result in your eliminating some articles simply because your library doesn't have them.

After you have compiled a list of books and articles which should be in your library, check to see if they really are on the shelves. You may find that some are checked out to other students or simply missing. This is a good time to scan your sources to get some idea of their usefulness. Examine the tables of contents and indexes of books. You may find that a source on your list contains much—or nothing—about your subject.

Some researchers find the *annotated* working bibliography to be a timesaver. An annotation is a brief note to yourself about what a book or an article contains. Example:

```
Gibson, Priscilla. "Dickens's Use of

    Animism." Nineteenth Century Fiction,

    7 (1953), 283-91.

    Interesting article on use of images to

    bring characters to life. Contains good

    examples.
```

Such annotations may be made as you scan your sources. If you plan to annotate, leave spaces between entries when you compile your working bibliography or else list titles on separate note cards.

Putting your hands on the books and articles at this point serves two purposes: (1) It enables you to find out if they are really available for use, and (2) it enables you to see what information they contain. This is also a good time to check out books which show potential.

Step 3: Narrow your topic.

Using your emended working bibliography, do some preliminary reading from your sources in order to limit your general subject to a specific area you wish to explore.

Beware: Resist the temptation to begin taking notes at this point. Most of the notes taken before you have narrowed your topic will only have to be discarded later—or, should you try to use them, will result in a poorly organized paper.

To exemplify this topic-narrowing process, the general subject of Dickens' novels may be reduced to Dickens' interesting characters and then, after some reading on the subject, to the tentative topic of how and why these characters continue to fascinate readers. You may visualize this topic-narrowing process as an inverted pyramid:

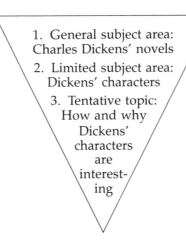

1. General subject area: Charles Dickens' novels
2. Limited subject area: Dickens' characters
3. Tentative topic: How and why Dickens' characters are interesting

Step 4: Take notes.

Read through your sources again and carefully select information related to your specific topic. (You do not need to read entire books. Use the table of contents and index to identify the parts on your subject.) Write the information on note cards.

If you find that the sources in your working bibliography are inadequate, you must explore additional sources or change your topic. A paper based on only a few sources is more of a synopsis than a research paper.

To ensure a well-organized paper, don't write notes in a notebook, don't write more than one note on a card, and don't write notes on both sides of cards. Use 4 × 6 note cards. The 3 × 5 cards do not provide adequate space, and the 5 × 8 cards encourage wordiness and are hard to manipulate. Be sure to write the author's name and the page number of the quotation or paraphrase at the top of the card. (Full bibliographical information should be contained in your working bibliography.) Save the note cards because you may be required to turn them in with the completed paper.

If two or more of your books or articles are by the same author, you must note the title, as well as the author, at the top of the card. Suppose your sources include T. S. Eliot's article "In Memoriam" and Eliot's book *The Sacred Wood.* To distinguish which source a note is taken from, you would write, for instance, Eliot, "In Memoriam," p. 214 at the top of one card and Eliot, *The Sacred Wood,* p. 96 at the top of another. Eliot, p. 214 would not identify which source the quotation is from. In footnotes, you would, of course, give full information on both sources the first time you use them in your paper.

When you footnote more than one work by the same author, titles are needed in addition to names in subsequent references. (A subsequent reference is a shortened footnote used after you have given full information in the first reference. See examples beginning on p. 138.) If two of your authors have the same last name, give both first and last names on note cards and in subsequent references. Example:

³T. S. Eliot, p. 73.

⁴George Eliot, p. 207.

You must be especially careful in taking notes. Copy quotations accurately—down to the last comma. You should have no errors due to miscopying of notes.

Make your notes as brief as possible. Instead of copying a lengthy passage, select the key sentence or sentences stating the gist of its thought. When quoting word for word, use the ellipsis (. . .) to omit irrelevant material. When you use the ellipsis to eliminate part of a sentence, make sure that the retained words still make a grammatical sentence. You can't change any of the wording of a direct quotation, but, when necessary, you may add your own words within quotations by using brackets [like this]. Always place directly quoted material within quotation marks on your note cards to distinguish it from paraphrased material.

Paraphrase—stating someone else's thought in your own words and style—is a means of reducing researched material to its essence. It is also a way of getting your own "voice" into a research paper. Furthermore, successful paraphrase indicates that you have understood and absorbed the ideas of the authorities you have consulted (a virtue that a paper of strung-together quotations does not exhibit). To avoid the "patchwork quilt" effect produced by too many direct quotations, include a lot of paraphrases in your research paper. Some writers believe that the only time a researched idea should *not* be paraphrased is when the wording of the original is particularly significant. *But remember: Paraphrases, as well as direct quotations, must be footnoted.*

The pitfall of paraphrasing is that it can lead to plagiarism unless you are scrupulously careful. Contrary to popular misconception, changing a few words or even most of the wording of the original does not constitute acceptable paraphrase. A paraphrase must be expressed *completely* in your own words and in a sentence structure different from that of the original source.

Therefore, in paraphrasing on note cards, you should read the original passage carefully, close the book, wait a few moments, then write down the idea in your own words. Next, match the paraphrase against the original to make sure that you have not unconsciously preserved its sentence structure or inadvertently repeated key words or phrases. If the sentence structure of your paraphrase is essentially the same as the original, try again. If key words or phrases have been repeated, put quotation marks around them—or, better still, substitute synonyms for these words. You should follow the same conversion procedure if you decide to change a direct quotation on a note card to a paraphrase within your paper.

To distinguish paraphrases from direct quotations, do not put quotation marks around paraphrases, either on note cards or in your paper. Make sure, however, that there is no direct quoting in a passage without quotation marks. A mishandled "paraphrase" on a note card will show up as a plagiarized passage if used in your paper. Remember that while you should have no quotation marks around a paraphrase, you still must footnote the source of the idea. (See Plagiarism, p. 332.)

Here are samples of the three types of notes as they would appear on note cards:

1. Word-for-word quotation:

> Buckley, p. 60
> "Ulysses is driven,
> Faust—like, to follow
> endlessly unsatisfied desire
> as a good in itself."

2. Paraphrase:

> Buckley, p. 60
> Ulysses is a restless character
> interested only in
> self—gratification.

3. Direct quotation and paraphrase combined:

> Buckley, p. 60
> Ulysses is a "Faust—like"
> character interested only in
> self—gratification "as a good
> in itself."

Since none of these notes represents the research writer's original thought, each would be followed by a footnote number if used in a paper.

Step 5: Organize notes under major headings.

Carefully examine your notes and arrange them in various stacks according to their main ideas. As a preliminary to this step, some writers jot the main idea of a note at the top of the card.

In sorting your note cards, don't force an idea into a category of thought which it really doesn't fit. Cards which do not fit into any of the large stacks should be set aside. If you have taken notes wisely, you will be able to get the organization, or the main points, of your paper from these different stacks of cards.

You should not, of course, attempt to use every stack of cards. Retain only those groupings which fit together into a logical sequence of thought. Upon examination, you may find that two or three stacks with few cards will combine to form a new part of your paper under a new heading. Nevertheless, you must eliminate whole stacks, no matter how many cards they contain, if they do not tie in with the gist of the paper which is beginning to take shape.

Step 6: Formulate the thesis of your paper.

Examine your working note cards (those selected in Step 5) and from them deduce a thesis, or controlling idea, for your paper. For the sample research paper which follows, the topic of how and why Charles Dickens' characters are interesting was further limited to this thesis: They are fascinating because they are real and believable, but also overstated just enough to make them unique and memorable. A formal statement of your thesis should appear in the introductory paragraph of your paper, and all the information of the paper must be focused upon it.

This final narrowing of the topic into a thesis statement is absolutely essential. An in-depth examination of a limited topic makes a much better paper than does a sketchy commentary on a broad topic.

Step 7: Order the main points and make an outline.

Arrange your selected stacks of note cards in the sequence which best develops your thesis. This will give you the main points of your paper in the order in which they will be presented. List these main points, along with your thesis statement, on a separate sheet of paper. Even if your instructor does not call for a formal outline, this step is necessary if your paper is to be organized. Example:

```
Charles Dickens' Characterization


Thesis: The great majority of Dickens'

characters are fascinating and believable

people, drawn just a little larger than life

to make them memorable.

    I.  Most memorable types

        A.  Burlesque

        B.  Satirical
```

II. Close observation

    A. London life

    B. First impressions

III. Characterizing names

    A. Punning

    B. Literal

    C. Unusual

    D. Showing hatred of lawyers

    E. Showing sympathy for lower classes

    F. Subtle

    G. Carefully selected

IV. Characterizing dialogue

    A. Mrs. Micawber

    B. Mr. Micawber

    C. Mrs. Gradgrind

    D. Mrs. Joe and Pumblechook

V. Characterizing imagery

    A. Inanimate as animate

    B. Animate as inanimate

    C. Animal images

```
        D.  Images of environment and

            possessions

    VI. The debate over Dickens'

        characterization

        A.  Villains

        B.  Heroes and heroines

        C.  Realistic or caricatures?
```

Step 8: Write a first draft.

In writing the paper, take your information point by point, select your best note cards under each heading, and, as you write, rearrange them and tie them together in a logical sequence of thought. Whereas a shorter paper usually has one paragraph for each main point, a research paper usually requires several paragraphs of development for each main point.

To facilitate this selecting process, spread out before you all the notes retained on the point being developed. This will enable you to select your best notes and incorporate them into the paper in the most effective order.

As you select notes to fit your developing line of thought, you will be eliminating many which you earlier thought you might use. Writing an effective research paper is a process of narrowing and selecting. If you use all or even most of the notes you have taken, the resulting paper will almost certainly be repetitious or poorly focused on your thesis. Select the very best ideas gleaned from your sources, and eliminate all notes which are not closely related to your thesis or which repeat a point better stated in another note. In this manner, you reduce the ideas retained in your paper to the best of what your sources say on the topic.

As you write the first draft, be sure to introduce all quotations and paraphrases, and smoothly incorporate them into the flow of the paper. Analyze, explain, and relate these researched ideas to your thesis and offer your own ideas where appropriate. *As you write, list on a separate page the sources quoted or paraphrased, with numbers corresponding to the reference numbers within your paper.*

You must, of course, follow the stylistic conventions of research writing as exemplified by the sample research papers beginning on p. 152. Before beginning the first draft, you may also find it useful to examine the checklist in the next step.

Step 9: Edit and revise.

Before typing a final copy, put your paper through at least two drafts, polishing the style and tightening the relationship of ideas. Many writers find it convenient to compose the first draft in longhand rather than at the typewriter. If your instructor specifies a certain length for the paper, you may gauge the length of your typed paper by composing the rough draft in a legal-size notebook. One page of normal handwriting in this size notebook roughly corresponds to one page of double-spaced typing. Expand or reduce your rough draft accordingly to meet specified length. Writing a paper much shorter or much longer than the prescribed limits will usually count against you.

While the paper is still in rough-draft form, check it against the following list:

1. Have you given credit, in the form of footnotes, for all

ideas taken from your sources, even if they are paraphrased and not quoted?

2. Have you given credit, in the form of footnotes *and* quotation marks, for all wording repeated from your sources, even if it is only a phrase or a key word?

3. Have you properly introduced and incorporated all quotations? These are some of the common methods of handling quotations:

   a. According to Jerome Buckley, "Ulysses is driven, Faust-like, to follow endlessly unsatisfied desire as a good in itself."[10]

      Note the comma after the introductory phrase "According to Jerome Buckley." There also would be a comma after "Jerome Buckley says," in introducing a quotation.

   b. Jerome Buckley says that "Ulysses is driven, Faust-like, to follow endlessly unsatisfied desire as a good in itself."[10]

      In this type of sentence, "that" replaces the comma after the identifying remark.

   c. Jerome Buckley considers Ulysses a restless man enslaved by selfishness: "Ulysses is driven, Faust-like, to follow endlessly unsatisfied desire as a good in itself."[10]

      Note that when the introductory remark is a statement, it is followed by a colon and not a comma.

   d. Instead of being formally introduced, a quotation may be incorporated as part of a sentence written by the research writer: The Ulysses who "is driven, Faust-like, to follow endlessly unsatisfied desire as a good in itself"[10] may represent Tennyson's desire to flee from a life of duty.

Note that the footnote number comes at the end of the quotation, not the end of the sentence. For a combination quotation and paraphrase, the footnote number comes at the end of the sentence in order to cover both: Ulysses pursues "endlessly unsatisfied desire," much like another egotist, Faust. [10]

4. Have you introduced all paraphrases to show where they begin? Since paraphrases are not enclosed in quotation marks, it usually is impossible to tell where a paraphrase begins unless it is introduced in some manner. Suppose, for instance, that the following passage appeared in a research paper:

> On the surface, Tennyson's Ulysses seems to be a noble man of action. Victorians may have considered Ulysses a heroic figure, but he is really a restless character interested only in self-gratification. [10]

It is impossible to tell if both statements preceding the footnote number are paraphrased, the second statement only, or just the last part of the second statement. Compare:

> On the surface, Tennyson's Ulysses seems to be a noble man of action. Victorians may have considered Ulysses a heroic figure, but Jerome Buckley sees him as a restless character interested only in self-gratification. [10]

The reference to Buckley in this version makes it clear that only the last idea of the passage is paraphrased. This reference indicates where the paraphrase begins, and the footnote number shows where it ends. Always introduce your paraphrases by mentioning the source and follow them with a footnote number.

Never write several paraphrased sentences in a row and stick a footnote number after them, with no incorporated references to the sources. Furthermore, never allow a paraphrase from a single source to run as long as a paragraph in your paper.

5. Can any lengthy quotations be reduced by means of ellipsis or paraphrase without loss of necessary information or distinctive phrasing?

   Lengthy quotations must be indented, or blocked, in the paper. Quotations long enough to require indentation should be held to a minimum. But when lengthy quotations are necessary, this rule must be followed: Prose quotations running five typed lines or more and poetry quotations running four lines or more must be indented. (See quotation number three in the first sample research paper on p. 157–58 for an example.) Indented quotations are not enclosed by quotation marks unless quotation marks appear in the original (as in dialogue or a statement which is also quoted in your source).

6. Have you completely reshaped the ideas of your sources into your own sequence of thought or have you merely transcribed chunks of researched material into your paper? You have committed the error of too much consecutive quoting if any of your footnotes look like this:

6Eliot, p. 214.

7Eliot, p. 216.

8Eliot, p. 217.

9Eliot, p. 215.

If you have digested and reshaped your researched material, the references to your various sources will be mixed together throughout the paper and will not appear in blocks as in the preceding example.

Nor should any of your footnotes look like this: 6Eliot, pp. 207–11. Such a footnote indicates either a too-lengthy paraphrase or an inaccurate identification of the *exact* source of the idea. Virtually the only time a reference should cover more than one page is when an idea begins at the bottom of one page of a source and continues to the top of the next, in which case the footnote would look like this: 6Eliot, pp. 207–08. Reference to more than two pages is careless research technique.

7. Have you maintained a balance between your own comments and the ideas from your sources? Remember that your own writing should be *interwoven* with source material throughout the paper. Watch out for several footnoted passages bunched together, even if they are from different sources.

8. Do your footnotes conform exactly to the models beginning on p. 137? Have you followed the correct form for subsequent references?

9. Have you listed any source in your bibliography which

is not footnoted in the paper? (If so, omit it.) Is the bibliography alphabetized by authors' last names (or by first important word of title if no author is given)? Do the entries conform exactly to the models beginning on p. 138?

10. Is the paper tightly organized? Have you stuck strictly to proving the thesis? Do all the parts of the paper fit together logically—main point to main point, paragraph to paragraph, and sentence to sentence? If not, eliminate irrelevancies and rearrange for unity.

11. Have you eliminated all mechanical errors possible—grammar, punctuation, spelling?

Step 10: Write another draft.

In this version, incorporate all the corrections and revisions you have made on the previous draft, and improve the paper's style in any way you can. Most instructors require that research papers be typed. In typing, you should observe these conventions:

1. *Margins, pagination, and spacing.* Leave one-inch margins all around, except for two inches at the top of the first page of the paper and the first page of endnotes and bibliography. Begin numbering the pages with 2 on the second page of text in the upper right corner. Except as noted below, double-space throughout the paper.

2. *Indented quotations.* Block all quotations of five lines or more by indenting them ten spaces from the left margin. Double-space within these quotations and triple-space before and after them.

3. *Footnotes.* Quadruple-space before beginning footnotes at the bottom of the page, single-space within each entry, and double-space between footnotes. Indent the

first line of each footnote five spaces and number foot-notes consecutively throughout the paper.

4. *Endnotes* (alternative to footnotes). If you are permitted to document your paper at the end, come down two inches from the top of the first page of notes and head it "Notes." Quadruple-space after the heading. Indent the first line of each note five spaces and double-space within and between entries. Number notes consecutively to correspond to the numbers within the paper.

5. *Bibliography.* Using your footnotes or endnotes, make a list of the sources you have quoted or paraphrased in your paper. Alphabetize by author's last name or, if no name is given, by the first word of the title (excluding "a," "an," and "the"). Come down two inches from the top of the page and head this list "Bibliography." Quadruple-space after the heading. After the first line of each entry, indent all lines five spaces. Double-space within and between entries.

Step 11: Assemble the parts in the proper order.

1. Title page. There are many types of title page, and your instructor may tell you what information to include. Otherwise, you may use this form:

```
                    Title of Paper




                    Your name

                    Course title

               Term and year of class
```

2. Outline (if you are required to turn one in)
3. Text of paper
4. Notes (if footnotes are not used)
5. Bibliography

Before turning in the paper, give it one final proofreading. Most instructors permit neatly erased and printed-in corrections on the final copy. (Use dark ink.) Numerous or major corrections, however, necessitate retyping.

Step 12: Proofread again and add final touches.

Be sure to fasten the paper together. Do not place the paper in a binder unless you are specifically required to do so. Instead, staple the pages at the upper left corner for ease in reading.

SAMPLE FOOTNOTES AND BIBLIOGRAPHY ENTRIES

Book by a Single Author

[1]Jerome Buckley, <u>Tennyson</u>: The <u>Growth</u> <u>of</u> <u>a</u> <u>Poet</u> (Cambridge, Massachusetts: Harvard University Press, 1960), p. 53.

[Author, <u>Title</u> (Place of Publication: Publisher, date of publication), page number of reference.]

Subsequent reference (any reference to a source after it has been fully footnoted the first time it is cited):

```
2Buckley, p. 37.
```

Use this short form for footnoting any source which has been fully documented in a previous footnote or endnote. The author's last name and page number are clearer and more informative than are the Latin abbreviations "ibid." and "op. cit." for subsequent references.

If, however, you have previously footnoted *two* works by the same author, in subsequent references you must give the short title of the work—in addition to author and page number—to distinguish between the two works. Suppose, for instance, that you have previously footnoted *Tennyson: The Growth of a Poet* and *The Victorian Temper: A Study in Literary Culture*, both by Jerome Buckley. Subsequent references would look like this:

```
9Buckley, Tennyson, p. 12.

16Buckley, The Victorian Temper, p. 33.
```

Bibliography:

```
Buckley, Jerome. Tennyson: The Growth of a
     Poet. Cambridge, Massachusetts: Harvard
     University Press, 1960.
```

Book by Two Authors

³Rexford Collingwood and Fredson Bushnell, The Lofty Victorians (London: Farthing Press, 1917), pp. 17–18.

Subsequent reference:

⁴Collingwood and Bushnell, p. 223.

Bibliography:

Collingwood, Rexford, and Fredson Bushnell. The Lofty Victorians. London: Farthing Press, 1917.

Book by More Than Two Authors

⁵Edmond Gross and others, Tennyson and the Changing Critical Climate (Liverpool: Parham Books, 1952), p. 6.

Subsequent reference:

⁶Gross and others, p. 97.

Bibliography:

Gross, Edmond, and others. <u>Tennyson</u> <u>and</u> <u>the</u>
      <u>Changing</u> <u>Critical</u> <u>Climate</u>. Liverpool:
      Parham Books, 1952.

Edited Anthology of the Writings of a Single Author

      [7]Alfred Tennyson, <u>The</u> <u>Poetic</u> <u>and</u>
<u>Dramatic</u> <u>Works</u> <u>of</u> <u>Alfred</u> <u>Lord</u> <u>Tennyson</u>, ed.
W.J. Rolfe (Boston: Houghton Mifflin,
1898), "Ulysses," l. 70, p. 89.

Subsequent reference:

      [8]Tennyson, "Teresias," ll. 28–29,
p. 490.

   If a collection or a single literary work is to be used extensively throughout a paper, subsequent references to it are usually placed within parentheses after the quotations. A note to the effect that subsequent references will be incorporated into the text of the paper is appended to the first full footnote on the source. Example: All future references to Tennyson's poems are to this edition and are incorporated into the text of the paper.

When literary works are cited in parentheses within a paper, these conventions ordinarily are followed:

1. Reference to a poem:

   ("Ulysses," l. 9).

   [Poem title and line number of quotation.] Use ll. for more than one line:

   ("Ulysses," ll. 9–10).

2. Reference to a play:

   (Becket, v, ii, 19–20).

   [Title, act, scene, lines if numbered in play; page number if not.]

3. Reference to a short story:

   ("Ethan Brand," p. 72).

   [Title and page number only.]

4. Reference to a novel:

   (Dr. Jekyll and Mr. Hyde, p. 13).

   [Title and page number.]

Titles usually are omitted from references within parentheses if the introduction of the quotation names or otherwise clearly indicates the work quoted from.

For incorporated references, place sentence punctuation (usually a period) after the parentheses unless the quotation is indented, in which case sentence punctuation is placed before the parenthetical reference.

Bibliography:

Tennyson, Alfred. <u>The</u> <u>Poetic</u> <u>and</u> <u>Dramatic</u> <u>Works</u> <u>of</u> <u>Alfred</u> <u>Lord</u> <u>Tennyson</u>. Ed. W.J. Rolfe. Boston: Houghton Mifflin, 1898.

Edited Anthology of the Works of Several Authors

[9]Walter E. Houghton and G. Robert Stange, eds., <u>Victorian</u> <u>Poetry</u> <u>and</u> <u>Poetics</u> (Boston: Houghton Mifflin, 1959), p. 5.

Subsequent reference:

[10]Houghton and Stange, p. 20.

Bibliography:

Houghton, Walter E., and G. Robert Stange, eds. <u>Victorian</u> <u>Poetry</u> <u>and</u> <u>Poetics</u>. Boston: Houghton Mifflin, 1959.

Essay in an Edited Collection

[11]Arthur J. Carr, "Tennyson as a Modern Poet," in Critical Essays on the Poetry of Tennyson, ed. John Killham (New York: Barnes and Noble, 1960), p. 41.

Subsequent reference:

[12]Carr, p. 55.

Bibliography:

Carr, Arthur J. "Tennyson as a Modern Poet." In Critical Essays on the Poetry of Tennyson, ed. John Killham. New York: Barnes and Noble, 1960.

Work of More Than One Volume

[13]Hallam Tennyson, Alfred Lord Tennyson: A Memoir (London: Macmillan, 1897), I, 196.

Subsequent reference:

[14]Tennyson, 193.

Bibliography:

Tennyson, Hallam. <u>Alfred</u> <u>Lord</u> <u>Tennyson</u>: <u>A</u>

    <u>Memoir</u>. Vol. I. London: Macmillan, 1897.

Bound Magazine or Journal Article with Continuous Page Numbering

    [15]Warren Beck, "Clouds Upon Camelot,"

<u>English</u> <u>Journal</u>, 45 (1956), 448.

Note: The volume numbers of some journals are in roman numerals. If you need assistance in converting roman to arabic numbers, consult the conversion table in your dictionary (usually under "roman numeral" or "number").

    [16]Beck, 450.

Bibliography:

Beck, Warren. "Clouds Upon Camelot." <u>English</u>

    <u>Journal</u>, 45 (1956), 447–54, 503.

Note that the bibliography entry gives the *total* number of pages of the article. Beck's article begins on page 447 and runs through page 454, then is continued and ended on page 503.

Bound Magazine or Journal Article with Issues Numbered Separately

[17]C.A. Bodelsen, "The Physiognomy of the Name," Review of English Literature, 2, No. 3 (1961), 46.

Subsequent reference:

[18]Bodelsen, 43.

Bibliography:

Bodelsen, C.A. "The Physiognomy of the Name." Review of English Literature, 2, No. 3 (1961), 39–48.

Note that when a collected article is numbered separately, the issue number is given (in addition to the volume number and year) in both footnote and bibliography entries.

Single Unbound Issue of a Magazine or Journal

[19]Julia Kell, "Shades of Queen Victoria," Time, 2 Jan. 1975, p. 93.

Subsequent reference:

    [20]Kell, p. 94.

Bibliography:

Kell, Julia. "Shades of Queen Victoria."

    Time, 2 Jan. 1975, pp. 93–94.

Note that the bibliography lists total pages of both bound and unbound articles.

Newspaper Article

    [21]"An Unpublished Poem by Tennyson,"

Toledo Double-Dealer, 13 Sept. 1962,

sec. D, p. 28.

Subsequent reference:

    [22]"An Unpublished Poem by Tennyson,"

p. 28.

Bibliography:

"An Unpublished Poem by Tennyson." Toledo

Double-Dealer, 13 Sept. 1962, sec. D, p.
28.

Encyclopedia Article

[23]"Alfred Lord Tennyson," Encyclopedia
Britannica, 1974 ed., XVIII, 141.

Subsequent reference:

[24]"Alfred Lord Tennyson," XVIII, 140.

Bibliography:

"Alfred Lord Tennyson." Encyclopedia
        Britannica, 1974 ed.

Note: Most newspaper and encyclopedia articles (and many magazine articles) are unsigned. If no author is given, begin footnotes with titles, as illustrated above. In the bibliography, unsigned entries are alphabetized by the first word of the title (excluding "a," "an," and "the").

Pamphlet

a.   [25]Woodrow Allenstein, Government
    Subsidy of the Arts (Greenwich Village:

Society for Preservation of Aesthetics,
1967), p. 9.

Subsequent reference:

26Allenstein, p. 83.

Bibliography:

Allenstein, Woodrow. Government Subsidy of
        the Arts. Greenwich Village: Society for
        Preservation of Aesthetics, 1967.

b.   27Department of Library Science, A Guide
    to the Library (Boone, North Carolina:
    Appalachian Press, 1930), p. 16.

Subsequent reference:

28A Guide to the Library, p. 101.

Bibliography:

Department of Library Science. A Guide to the

Library. Boone, North Carolina:
Appalachian Press, 1930.

c.   [29]U.S. Department of Health, Education,
and Welfare, A History of the WPA
(Washington, D.C.: Government Printing
Office, 1963), p. 37.

Subsequent reference:

[30]A History of the WPA, p. 18.

Bibliography:

U.S. Department of Health, Education, and
Welfare. A History of the WPA.
Washington, D.C.: Government Printing
Office, 1963.

Interview

[31]Interview with Sir Kingsley Trump,
curator of the Museum of Victorian
Artifacts, Cambridge, Massachusetts,
6 Jan. 1976.

Subsequent reference:

> [32]Trump, interview.

Bibliography:

Trump, Sir Kingsley. Interview. Cambridge,
> Massachusetts, 6 Jan. 1976.

Lecture

> [33]Professor J. Allen Rice, Modern Poetry
Lecture, University of North Carolina,
Chapel Hill, Spring Semester, 1973.

Subsequent reference:

> [34]Rice, lecture.

Bibliography:

Rice, Professor J. Allen. Modern Poetry
> Lecture. University of North Carolina,
> Chapel Hill, Spring Semester, 1973.

Broadcast Statement

```
  35Eric Sevareid, CBS Evening News,
7 Dec. 1978.
```

Subsequent reference:

```
  36Sevareid, newscast.
```

Bibliography:

```
Sevareid, Eric. CBS Evening News. 7 Dec.
    1978.
```

SAMPLE RESEARCH PAPERS

Many instructors prefer undergraduate research papers to be short and concise. You must show some thought on your subject, but in a beginning writing class you are not expected to do sophisticated research and arrive at original conclusions. The freshman research paper is primarily an exercise in technique.

A short research paper will familiarize you with library resources and give you practice in correct use and documentation of researched ideas. Following are two such papers. The first is on a literary topic and has footnotes. The second is on a topic of general interest with notes at the end.

The Lively Throng: Charles Dickens' Ingenious

Characterization

Amy Scott

English 101

Spring Semester 1980

Thesis: The great majority of Dickens'
characters are fascinating and believable
people, drawn just a little larger than life
to make them memorable.

   I. Most memorable types

      A. Burlesque

      B. Satirical

  II. Close observation

      A. London life

      B. First impressions

III. Characterizing names

      A. Punning

      B. Literal

      C. Unusual

      D. Showing hatred of lawyers

      E. Showing sympathy for lower classes

      F. Subtle

      G. Carefully selected

IV. Characterizing dialogue

    A. Mrs. Micawber

    B. Mr. Micawber

    C. Mrs. Gradgrind

    D. Mrs. Joe and Pumblechook

 V. Characterizing imagery

    A. Inanimate as animate

    B. Animate as inanimate

    C. Animal images

    D. Images of environment and possessions

VI. The debate over Dickens' characterization

    A. Villains

    B. Heroes and heroines

    C. Realistic or caricatures?

The Lively Throng: Charles Dickens'
Ingenious Characterization

Literary critics argue a great deal about
Dickens' characters. Many dismiss them as
unbelievable grotesques, while others praise
them for their uniqueness. Close examination
reveals that the greatest English novelist of
the nineteenth century endowed the multitudes
who populate his fictional world with their
own brand of heightened realism. The great
majority of Dickens' characters are
fascinating and believable people, drawn just
a little larger than life to make them
memorable.

Dickens' characters are uniquely
individualistic, but the most memorable ones
fall into two broad categories. Both types
are comic, but comic in two very different
ways. David Daiches says that Dickens "never

lost his touch for burlesque or for satiric comedy."[1] Dickens' love of comedy led him to burlesque many of his characters and to laugh at them in a good-natured way. On the other hand, his hatred of evil and oppression compelled him to satirize his less noble creations. Both types are present in Dickens' second publication, and his first important one, the Pickwick Papers (1836–37). The burlesque figures are best represented by the innocent idealist Mr. Pickwick and the comic servant Sam Weller. According to Walter Allen, the Pickwick Papers, which came out in monthly installments, increased greatly in popularity when Sam Weller was introduced in the fifth issue.[2] Dickens laughs at Mr.

[1]David Daiches, A Critical History of English Literature (New York: Ronald Press, 1960), II, 1052.

[2]Walter Allen, Six Great Novelists (London: H. Hamilton, 1955), p. 107.

Pickwick, Sam Weller, and the other naive
Pickwickians, but it is clear that he finds
them charming and supports them all the way.
The satirical figures, best represented by
Dodson and Fogg, prototypes of the lawyers
Dickens despised, are another matter. Dickens
typically treats such characters with ironic,
contemptuous humor. He dislikes these
characters and plainly wants his readers to
dislike them too.

Whether Dickens is for or against a
character, his creations are almost always
memorable and interesting. Dickens was always
on the lookout for a revealing character
trait. Living in London, he closely observed
the world around him and used much of what he
saw in his writing. Dickens once wrote in a
letter to a friend:

> We revel in a crowd of any kind—a
> street "row" [commotion] is our

delight--even a woman in a fit is by
no means to be despised, especially
in a fourth-rate street, where all
the female inhabitants run out of
their houses. . . . Then a drunken
man--what can be more charming than
a regular drunken man, who sits in a
doorway for half an hour, holding a
dialogue with the crowd?[3]

Such close observation apparently paid off.
G. K. Chesterton says that Dickens was "a man
of impressions; he has never been equalled in
the art of conveying what a man looks like at
first sight."[4]

[3]John Butt and Kathleen Tillotson,
Dickens at Work (Fair Lawn, N.J.: Essential
Books, 1958), p. 44.

[4]G. K. Chesterton, Appreciations and
Criticism of the Works of Charles Dickens
(London: Dent, 1911), p. xiii.

The names Dickens gives his characters are often a key to their personalities. "Bounderby," for example, is a play on "bounder," a popular British slang term for an overbearing, cloddish person. "Mrs. Havisham" is a fairly common name, but the fact that the old lady lives in a dreamworld suggests that Dickens may have had "have a sham" in mind. Dickens often uses such punning names, but many convey information literally, such as "Dr. Payne," "Lord Mutanhead," "The Artful Dodger," "The Aged," and "The Avenger." Also fairly obvious are the names given lighthearted, cheerful characters, such as "Cheeryble," "Trotwood," and "Peggoty," and to villains, like "Deadlock," "Slyme," "Veneering," "Grad-grind," and "Murdstone." The list of unforgettable names from Dickens is almost endless: "M'Chokumchild," "Pecksniff," "Pumblechook," "Wopsle," "Magwitch,"

"Scrooge," and even "Mealy Potatoes."
Dickens' hatred of lawyers is reflected in
such satirical names as "Tulkinghorn,"
"Conversation Kenge," "Jaggers," "Fogg," and
"Vholes." His pity for the miserable lower
classes is suggested by the ugly, one-
syllable names he assigned them, such as
"Knag," "Pott," "Slurk," and "Grub."

Most of Dickens' names speak for themselves, but some are rather subtle. Mrs.
Leo Hunter, for instance, hunts social lions,
implied by the first name "Leo." "Estella"
suggests "constellation," which perfectly
fits this cold, glittering character. C. A.
Bodelsen says that "Murdstone" connotes a
murderous hardness[5] and that the characterization of Inspector Bucket as
ordinary, but solid and dependable, is

[5]C. A. Bodelsen, "The Physiognomy of the
Name," Review of English Literature, 2,
No. 3 (1961), 46.

achieved by naming him after a "useful everyday household article."[6]

Dickens considered names a very important part of his characterization, and he worked hard at it. Sometimes he would modify a name until he got just the connotation he wanted. Harry Stone says that Dickens' manuscripts show that he toyed with "Hardle," "Murdle," and "Murden" before hitting upon "Murdstone" and that he worked through "Sweezleden," "Sweezleback," "Sweezlewag," "Chuzzletoe," "Chuzzleboy," and "Chuzzlewig" before arriving at "Chuzzlewit."[7] Stone also says that Dickens was constantly in search of unusual names and that he kept long lists gleaned from Privy Council Educational Reports. "Plornish," "Gargery," "Magwitch,"

---

[6]Bodelsen, 47.

[7]Harry Stone, "Dickens and the Naming of Sam Weller," The Dickensian, 56 (1960), 47.

"Wegg," "Podsnap," and "Dorrit" are just a
few which he got from such sources.[8] No matter
how Dickens arrived at his names, practically
every one seems perfectly fitted to the
personality of its bearer.

The fact that the sound of Dickens' names
is often an important part of their meaning
supports Angus Wilson's statement that
"Dickens' greatest natural gift was his
ear."[9] One way Dickens uses his ear--and
makes his readers use theirs--is by giving
some of his characters what Archibald
Coolidge calls "characteristic dialogue"
each time they appear.[10] Like some people in

[8]Stone, 47–48.

[9]Angus Wilson, "Dickens: A Haunting,"
Critical Quarterly, 2 (1960), 104.

[10]Archibald C. Coolidge, "Dickens's Use
of Character as Novelty," South Atlantic
Quarterly, 61 (1962), 407.

real life, these characters seem to be obsessed with certain expressions. In Dickens, these phrases usually emphasize a character's dominant personality trait. For instance, Mrs. Micawber nobly announces, again and again, that she will never leave Mr. Micawber. In turn, Mr. Micawber, the incurable optimist, is always sure "something will turn up." Mrs. Gradgrind knows that any minute something will be the death of her, and both Mrs. Joe and Pumblechook never let Pip forget that he was "brought up by hand." Such phrases indicate a single-mindedness bordering on obsession, and it is hard to forget Dickens' characters with such one-track minds.

Dickens' eye was just as keen as his ear. With heightened perception, he saw the world as alive with images, a feature which he sometimes made part of his characterization. As Priscilla Gibson points out, Dickens often

saw "the inanimate world as animated."[11]
Take, for example, this imagistic
description of Gradgrind:

> "Stick to the facts, Sir." The
> speaker's obstinate carriage,
> square coat, square legs, square
> shoulders--nay, his very neck-
> cloth, trained to take him by the
> throat with an unaccommodating grasp,
> like a stubborn fact as it were.[12]

Similarly, the unfeeling Jaggers "never
laughed; but . . . he sometimes caused his

[11]Priscilla Gibson, "Dickens's Use of
Animism," Nineteenth Century Fiction,
7 (1953), 283.

[12]Charles Dickens, Hard Times (London:
Nonesuch, 1937), p. 489.

boots to creak, as if they laughed in a dry
and suspicious way."[13]

Sometimes Dickens reverses the function
of his characterizing imagery and presents
the animate world as inanimate. Dorothy Van
Ghent mentions two excellent examples of
characters who have developed "thing-
attributes": "Podsnap, the capitalist,
who has hairbrushes on his head instead
of hair" and "the convict Magwitch,
mechanized by oppression and fear, who has
a clockwork apparatus in his throat, that
clicks as if it were going to strike."[14]

As R. D. McMaster has discovered, Dickens

[13]Charles Dickens, Great Expectations
(London: Nonesuch, 1937), p. 195.

[14]Dorothy Van Ghent, "The Dickens World:
A View From Todgers," Sewanee Review, 58
(1950), 420.

also makes brilliant use of animal images.[15]
For instance, James Carker, in <u>Dombey</u> <u>and</u>
<u>Son</u>, sports "Two unbroken rows of glistening
teeth whose regularity and whiteness were
quite distressing. . . . there was something
in [his smile] like the snarl of a cat."[16]
McMaster also notes that in <u>Nicholas</u>
<u>Nickleby</u>, Sir Mulburrey Hawk moves among
animallike creatures which include Mr. Pyke,
"a sharp-faced gentleman," and Mr. Snobb,
"with the neck of a stork and the legs of no
animal in particular."[17] In <u>Our</u> <u>Mutual</u>
<u>Friend</u>, Hexam is pictured as a vulture in a
"Dismal Swamp" full of "all manner of

[15]R. D. McMaster, "Man into Beast in
Dickensian Caricature," <u>University</u> <u>of</u>
<u>Toronto</u> <u>Quarterly</u>, 31 (1961-62), 356.

[16]Charles Dickens, <u>Dombey</u> <u>and</u> <u>Son</u>
(Boston: Houghton Mifflin, 1894), p. 179.

[17]Charles Dickens, <u>Nicholas</u> <u>Nickleby</u>
(Boston: Houghton Mifflin, 1894), p. 244.

crawling, creeping, fluttering and buzzing creatures."[18]

Such grotesque people reflect a morally sick environment. But, as Van Ghent says, the reverse is also true: Things, or environment, can reflect personality.[19] For example, the insect-infested wedding cake reveals Miss Havisham's sick mind. The crooked streets and slanting houses of Coketown are evidence of the wretchedness of the factory workers. Estelle's glittering jewels reflect her cold artificiality. The imaginary dust which Pip can't brush off is a sign of his feelings of guilt.

In spite of Dickens' firmly established place in literature, the critical debate over his characterization rages on. One common

[18]Charles Dickens, Our Mutual Friend (Boston: Houghton Mifflin, 1894), p. 220.

[19]Van Ghent, 421.

charge, even among critics who admit the vividness of Dickens' characters, is that his villains are simply too evil to be believable. Jared Wenger considers Dickens at his best in his portraits of murderers,[20] but Van Ghent says that Orlick, in Great Expectations, represents "all the undefined evil of the Dickens world" and that "Dickens does not try to 'psychologize' him through plotted cause and effect."[21] In other words, Van Ghent says that Orlick's evil is unmotivated. But it is possible that to Dickens the division between good and evil was clear-cut and that he believed evil people to be motivated simply by their evil natures. As George Santayana says, "His morose people were wicked, not virtuous in

[20]Jared Wenger, "Character-Types of Scott, Balzac, Dickens, Zola," PMLA, 62 (1947), 222.

[21]Van Ghent, 437.

their own way. . . . In him conscience was
single, and he could not conceive how it could
ever be divided in other men."[22]

Dickens obviously intended some of his
characters as one-sided villains, more
things than people. His sympathy for the
downtrodden led him to depict the oppressor
as a type, a symbol of the oppressive system.
Squeers, says Kenneth Fielding, is presented
not as a human being but as "the representative, pure and simple, of a vile
institution,"[23] the boys' boarding school.
Dickens's sympathy for the laboring class
caused him to type Bounderby as the symbol of
the factory system and Gradgrind as the
ultimate utilitarian. It is a measure of

[22]George Santayana, Essays in Literary
Criticism, ed. Irving Singer (New York:
Scribner's, 1956), pp. 212-13.

[23]Kenneth J. Fielding, Charles Dickens:
A Critical Introduction (Boston: Houghton
Mifflin, 1964), p. 39.

Dickens' genius that he managed to make even such villainous types memorable individuals.

Just as some critics argue that Dickens' villains are too villainous, others say that his heroes and heroines are too good to be true. This charge is more difficult to deny, possibly because perfect goodness is harder to believe than perfect evil. Van Ghent says, "As Orlick is one form of spiritual excess, Joe Gargery is the opposed form, unqualified love."[24] But if Joe were not depicted as somewhat simpleminded, his unwavering devotion to the ungrateful Pip would be incredible.

Probably because of his own unhappy childhood, Dickens had a special sympathy for youths, and his young heroes and heroines are generally his least successful characters.

[24]Van Ghent, 438.

With the exception of Pip, who is redeemed by human weakness, most of them are sentimentally drawn. Little Nell is Dickens' most notoriously maudlin portrait. But commenting on another virtuous heroine, Eugene Goodheart says, "If Uriah Heep is a monster of villainy, Ester Summerson is a monster of virtue."[25] Generally speaking, critics find Dickens' monsters of villainy more credible than his monsters of virtue, and all but the most sentimental readers would probably agree.

The argument over Dickens' characterization can be reduced to one basic question: Are they believable people or are they mere caricatures? Dickens certainly thought of them as real. He once stated that

[25]Eugene Goodheart, "Dickens's Method of Characterization," The Dickensian, 54 (1958), 35.

the main aim of a novelist was to present "speaking, moving human creatures,"[26] and his instructions to illustrators suggest that he had a definite mental image of his characters.[27] Some commentators, however, seem confused by Dickens' special brand of realism. George Orwell, for instance, calls Dickens' characters monsters, and then later in the same essay likens them to real people: "As with people one knew in childhood, one seems always to remember them in one particular attitude, doing one particular thing."[28] Perhaps the essence of Dickens' genius is that he captures the extraordinary features which make otherwise ordinary people interesting and memorable. Goodheart

[26]Quoted by Fielding, p. 109.

[27]Bodelsen, 40.

[28]George Orwell, _Critical Essays_ (London: Secker and Warburg, 1960), p. 53.

testifies to the realism even of Dickens'
one-sided characters by arguing that "most
human beings tend to be dominated by a single
trait or passion."[29] Santayana goes so far as
to say that the reader who cannot believe
Dickens' "ridiculous" characters is "a
pompous idealist who does not see the
ridiculous in all things"[30] and that "there
are such people; we are such people ourselves
in our true moments."[31] Yet it must be
admitted that even if Dickens' characters are
believable, most of them seem to be anything
but ordinary. As Walter Allen says,

> When we read Dickens, we soon
> realize that we are in the presence
> of anything but the common view of

[29]Goodheart, 35.

[30]Santayana, p. 221.

[31]Santayana, p. 217.

> life; we have been . . . plumped down
> at the center of a mind that sees
> and experiences life in a way quite
> other than that which we agree to
> think of as the normal, a mind that
> exists all the time at a pitch of
> intensity.[32]

Perhaps this is the most accurate view of
Dickens' characters: The great majority are
realistic, believable people drawn just a
little larger than life by the pen of a great
artist.

Even most of the critics who argue that
Dickens' characters lack realism admit that
these creations, so sharply defined by their
striking names, monomanic expressions, and
imagist descriptions, appear and reappear in
the reader's mind. Dickens' characters <u>live</u>,

[32]Allen, p. 109.

and readers continue to respond to them. As
G.K. Chesterton says,

> This is the first and last dignity of
> Dickens; that he was a creator. . . .
> We may disapprove of Mr. Guppy,
> but we recognize him as a creation
> flung down like a miracle out of an
> upper sphere; we can pull him to
> pieces, but we could not have put
> him together.[33]

If universal appeal is the main test of art,
then Dickens is a great artist on the strength
of his characters alone.

[33]G.K. Chesterton, <u>Charles Dickens</u>: <u>A
Critical Study</u> (New York: Dodd, Mead and
Company, 1906), pp. 244–45.

Bibliography

Allen, Walter. Six Great Novelists. London:

   H. Hamilton, 1955.

Bodelsen, C.A. "The Physiognomy of the Name."

   Review of English Literature, 2, No. 3

   (1961), 39-48.

Butt, John, and Kathleen Tillotson. Dickens

   at Work. Fair Lawn, N.J.: Essential

   Books, 1958.

Chesterton, G.K. Appreciations and Criticism

   of the Works of Charles Dickens. London:

   Dent, 1911.

_____ . Charles Dickens: A Critical Study.

   New York: Dodd, Mead and Company, 1906.

Coolidge, Archibald C. "Dickens's Use of

   Character as Novelty." South Atlantic

   Quarterly, 61 (1962), 405-10.

Daiches, David. A Critical History of English Literature. New York: Ronald Press, 1960. Vol. II.

Dickens, Charles. Dombey and Son. Boston: Houghton Mifflin, 1894.

———. Great Expectations. London: Nonesuch, 1937.

———. Hard Times. London: Nonesuch, 1937.

———. Nicholas Nickleby. Boston: Houghton Mifflin, 1894.

———. Our Mutual Friend. Boston: Houghton Mifflin, 1894.

Fielding, Kenneth J. Charles Dickens: A Critical Introduction. Boston: Houghton Mifflin, 1964.

Gibson, Priscilla. "Dickens's Use of Animism." Nineteenth Century Fiction, 7 (1953), 283–91.

Goodheart, Eugene. "Dickens's Method of Characterization." The Dickensian, 54 (1958), 35–37.

McMaster, R.D. "Man into Beast in Dickensian
Caricature." <u>University of Toronto
Quarterly</u>, 31 (1961–62), 354–61.

Orwell, George. <u>Critical Essays</u>. London:
Secker and Warburg, 1960.

Santayana, George. <u>Essays in Literary
Criticism</u>. Ed. Irving Singer. New York:
Scribner's, 1956.

Stone, Harry. "Dickens and the Naming of Sam
Weller." <u>The Dickensian</u>, 56 (1960),
47–49.

Van Ghent, Dorothy. "The Dickens World: A
View From Todgers." <u>Sewanee Review</u>, 58
(1950), 419–38.

Wenger, Jared. "Character–Types of Scott,
Balzac, Dickens, Zola." <u>PMLA</u>, 62 (1947),
213–32.

Wilson, Angus. "Dickens: A Haunting."
<u>Critical Quarterly</u>, 2 (1960), 101–08.

Goodbye, California

Suzanne Tise

English 100

Fall Semester 1980

Thesis: Unless science can discover
preventative measures, another severe
earthquake is likely to occur along the San
Andreas fault in the near future.

  I. Causes

      A. Locking plates

      B. Separating plates

      C. Nearby faults

  II. Damage

      A. To lives

      B. To property

III. Precautionary measures

      A. Release strain

      B. Predict and prepare

      C. Build quake-resistant structures

Goodbye, California

In 1906, San Francisco was shaken by a
violent earthquake that toppled buildings,
destroyed water lines, killed thousands of
people, and resulted in a fire that destroyed
half the city. There have been a number of
less severe earthquakes in Southern
California since then. These quakes are
caused by the strain which builds along the
San Andreas fault, a 650-mile-long and
thirty-mile-deep fracture in the earth's
crust. This pressure is accumulating again,
and seismologists predict that there will be
another major earthquake in the San Andreas
fault zone within this decade. Unless science
can discover preventative measures, this
prediction is almost certain to come true.

The underground strain which causes

earthquakes is created by the locking of the eight continental plates which make up the earth. Millions of years ago, these plates were joined together in one huge supercontinent. The plates eventually spread apart to their present positions. The San Andreas fault forms the dividing line between the North American plate and the Pacific Ocean plate. <u>Popular</u> <u>Science</u> <u>Monthly</u> states,

> As the plates slide and crunch by one another, they create a series of small tremors in most areas but keep moving. But in some areas they lock in place, and the strain builds for decades. When the rock finally breaks, it releases stored energy, shaking the earth and generating an earthquake.[1]

Unreleased pressure caused by these locked plates, calculated at 2 1/3 inches per year for the North Atlantic and Pacific Ocean plates, steadily builds to explosive proportions. Such is now the case in Southern California. Of the Palmdale bulge region, George Alexander says,

> Stress in the locked zone hasn't been dissipated at all. It has been building there for 119 years. At 2 1/3 inches per year, that's 278 inches of accumulated strain --approximately 23 feet of long overdue movement that will be made up in one sudden spastic movement when the subsurface rock layers finally yield.[2]

To put it simply, sooner or later this stored pressure has to be released. This fact not only makes another earthquake inevitable, but the longer the strain builds, the worse the quake will be.

Locked plates create the greatest hazard, but plates moving in the wrong direction can also be dangerous. Because the continental plates are lighter than the material below them, they move like a giant conveyor belt. Molten heat from the earth's interior rises to help support and carry the plates. However, Gribbin and Plagemann state in <u>The Jupiter Effect</u> that "a part of California to the east of the San Andreas fault is simply riding on a different plate from the rest of the USA" and that the Pacific Ocean plate is moving toward the north "at a rate of 3 1/3 to 5 cm [centimeters] per year."[3] A centimeter is .39 of an inch, and a movement of 1.4 to 1.9 inches per year may not seem like much. But the movement is in <u>different</u> directions, and, like the locked-in pressure, it builds over the years. As a result, a chunk of California may literally break off from the United States landmass.

Adding to the likelihood of a major quake, there are five other active faults in the San Francisco Bay region. Gordon Thomas and Max Witts have found that "the Hayward fault, just east of the San Andreas, is also looking dangerous. It runs across the campus and stadium of the University of Berkeley, where it is already causing damage."[4] Thomas and Witts also note that the San Francisco Bay Area Rapid Transit System and a major hospital are located on the Hayward fault,[5] thus increasing the potential loss of lives.

The main concern, of course, is the damage to both people and property that could be caused by a major earthquake. According to George Alexander, the Federal Disaster Relief Services Administration estimates that if a quake of magnitude 7.5 on the Richter Scale hit Los Angeles, it "could kill as many as 5000 people, injure upwards of 100,000 and cause $25 billion in property damages."[6]

California has more earthquake activity
than any other region in the continental
United States, and the chance of damage is
greatly increased by the dense population
of the southern part of the state. As the
Earthquake Information Bulletin reports,
"the Los Angeles earthquake of 1971
registered 6.6 on the Richter Scale, not a
major shock, but it occurred near a densely
populated area, causing damage estimated to
be near $448 million."[7] There is an even
greater earthquake risk in the San Francisco
Bay area, where an unusually large number of
hospitals and nursing homes are located.
Gribbin and Plagemann believe that if an
earthquake registering 8.3 on the Richter
Scale hit San Francisco, casualties would be
"nearly 1300 killed and 8000 injured" just in
the eighty-five hospitals in the area.[8]

Earthquakes are the hardest natural
disaster to contend with, according to

Gribbin and Plagemann, because of "their
indiscriminate effects and because they
provide no warning."[9] Once an earthquake
occurs, rescue work is especially difficult
because emergency relief centers usually are
destroyed and rescue workers are hampered by
the debris of fallen buildings. If a fire
resulted after a California earthquake, the
destruction could be greatly increased by the
dry winds there. Flooding caused by a severe
quake also would claim many lives.

Another disturbing factor is the risk of
disease. It could be weeks before all the dead
are dug out of the rubble. During that time,
the decaying bodies could breed disease of
epidemic proportions. Drinking water
polluted by broken sewage lines would greatly
increase sickness. Destruction of hospitals
would make quick treatment impossible.

Can anything be done to prevent such a
disaster? The Earthquake Information

<u>Bulletin</u> states that there are two possible
ways to release the strain along the San
Andreas fault. One is by small underground
nuclear explosions. If the explosions are not
carefully controlled, however, they could
trigger an earthquake in another country,
such as Russia, with disastrous political
results. The other possible remedy is to pump
fluid into the huge fault to set off harm—
less small earthquakes, thus releasing
accumulated strain.[10] However, such a mea—
sure would be very costly and, like the
underground explosions, would have to be
repeated as the strain builds again.

If earthquakes can't be prevented, at
least lives could be saved if the quakes could
be predicted. Geologists have identified some
signs which they hope will do just that.
Frequently, there are tremors, or tiny
earthquakes, before a major shock. But not
every small tremor is followed by a

high—magnitude earthquake, thus making this predictor unreliable. Prior to some past earthquakes, a change in the electrical conductivity of rocks has been noticed, along with tilting and bulging of the ground near the epicenter, which is the point directly above the place where the quake occurs inside the earth. The Chinese, before their earthquake in 1975, even noticed a drastic change in the behavior of animals. If a set of reliable predictors could be formulated, lives could be saved through evacuation. Earthquakes, however, remain very difficult to predict with certainty.

Some Californians have apparently resigned themselves to the inevitability of earthquakes and are concentrating on how to survive the shock rather than on how to prevent it. For instance, Alexander states that "the Los Angeles Building Department is pressing for passage of an ordinance that

would require owners of seismically
substandard buildings to rebuild them to meet
current safety standards or demolish them."[11]
Others are pushing for measures much broader
in scope. Karl Steinbrugge reports that

> large expenditures on earthquake
> research are being proposed by the
> scientific and engineering
> communities in the hope of
> predicting: 1) the occurrence of
> earthquakes, 2) the dynamic
> behavior of different kinds of
> ground, and 3) the dynamic behavior
> of various structures in relation
> to different kinds of ground.[12]

But such studies had better be completed and
their findings quickly put into practice. An
earthquake won't wait.

    When will the next earthquake occur? It

could be twenty years from now, next week, or tomorrow. The evidence shows that unless geologists can find a sure way to relieve the ever-mounting strain along the San Andreas fault, a major shock is inevitable. Gribbin and Plagemann make the terrifying prediction that in the near future "the Los Angeles region of the San Andreas fault will be subjected to the most massive earthquake known in the populated regions of the Earth in this century."[13] At the present, preventative measures seem beyond the knowledge of science. As a result, California could be headed for the worst natural disaster in our history.

Notes

[1]George Alexander, "Can We Predict the
Coming California Quake?" <u>Popular Science
Monthly</u>, 209, No. 5 (1976), 80.

[2]Alexander, 80.

[3]John R. Gribbin and Stephen Plagemann,
<u>The Jupiter Effect</u> (New York: Walker,
1974), p. 2.

[4]Gordon Thomas and Max Morgan Witts,
<u>The San Francisco Earthquake</u> (New York:
Stein and Day, 1971), p. 286.

[5]Thomas and Witts, p. 286.

[6]Alexander, 82.

[7]U.S. Department of the Interior,

Earthquake Information Bulletin
(Rockville, Maryland: Government Printing
Office, 1971), p. 15.

[8]Gribbin and Plagemann, p. 111.

[9]Gribbin and Plagemann, p. 108.

[10]Earthquake Information Bulletin,
p. 9.

[11]Alexander, 82.

[12]Karl V. Steinbrugge, Earthquake
Hazard in the San Francisco Bay Area
(Berkeley: Institute of Governmental
Studies, 1968), p. 1.

[13]Gribbin and Plagemann, p. 116.

Bibliography

Alexander, George. "Can We Predict the Coming
     California Quake?" Popular Science
     Monthly, 209, No. 5 (1976), 79–82.
Gribbin, John R., and Stephen Plagemann. The
     Jupiter Effect. New York: Walker, 1974.
Steinbrugge, Karl V. Earthquake Hazard in the
     San Francisco Bay Area. Berkeley:
     Institute of Governmental Studies,
     1968.
Thomas, Gordon, and Max Morgan Witts. The San
     Francisco Earthquake. New York: Stein
     and Day, 1971.
U.S. Department of the Interior. Earthquake
     Information Bulletin. Rockville,
     Maryland: Government Printing Office,
     1971.

4

Writing about Literature

One of my freshman students once apologized that she wasn't very good at reading things into literature. This statement reflects a common misconception about interpreting literature. The critical reader and writer should not read anything *into* literature but read *out of* literature the ideas the author put there for us to discover.

Another popular misconception is that these meanings are "hidden." Writers want to communicate. They don't want to hide their art or their meaning. The meaning and artistic beauty of a good piece of writing—whether it is fiction, poetry, or drama—are hidden only to the untrained eye. Furthermore, it does not take much training to find them, because in good literature the "hidden" or "deeper" meaning is very close to the surface, or literal level. The best interpretation, in fact, is the one which is most consistent with the obvious details of the story, poem, or play.

The aim of this chapter is to help you be a more perceptive reader—to read with a sharper eye, not to invent meanings which aren't there. In the sample essays which follow, you will see that the art and ideas of the selections analyzed are not hidden, but grow out of surface details and are quite accessible to the perceptive reader.

Becoming such a reader requires effort, but class discussion of literature provides training and practice. Class analysis of reading selections will help you learn how to interpret literature so that when a paper is assigned, you'll be able to put together an analysis on your own. You will write better papers about literature if you learn all you can about analytical reading by participating and being attentive to others' comments during class discussion of reading selections.

A critical paper is just a formally organized expression of an interpretation. Class discussions sometimes ramble, hit dead ends, or touch on minor features of a selection. This is all part of the learning process. The basic difference between discussing and writing is that when you write the final draft of an analysis paper, you are not in the process of discovering meaning but are putting into clear, organized form something of importance which you *have discovered* about a work of literature. As in other types of essays, you should include only ideas which develop your thesis (see Thesis Statements, p. 364), and you should support and illustrate those ideas with details.

You must be careful to achieve the right balance between interpretive ideas and supporting details. Facts from the literature are necessary, but they should be subordinated to your interpretation. They're your way of saying "I arrived at this particular meaning because of these things in the selection." Such specifics are a check to prevent you from venturing outside the work of literature into ideas which aren't there (reading into instead of out of), and they also show your reader your interpretation is based on solid evidence. These details both illustrate and justify your analysis. When the connection is not obvious, briefly explain how the particulars you have selected support your interpretation. The sample essays in this chapter illustrate how to interweave interpretive ideas with supporting details from the work being discussed.

SHORT STORY ANALYSIS

Most literature has three basic elements: (1) plot—the events, or story line; (2) character—the people involved in the events and affected by them; and (3) theme—what the work of literature says (the underlying idea about life or human nature which is illustrated by the interaction of character and event).

The beginning student of literature is apt to overemphasize plot simply because the story line is the most obvious component of literature. Except in pure adventure stories, however, the literal action is not especially significant. In most serious literature, a summary of the plot reveals almost nothing about meaning or character. Many stories, in fact, have very little overt action at all.

The first task in writing genuine literary analysis, then, is to learn to go beyond mere plot to the essential features of a piece of writing. Plot, of course, is a necessary element of fiction and drama, and it cannot be ignored. In literary analysis, however, plot should never be mentioned except to illustrate your interpretation—the emphasis must be upon your analysis of meaning and not upon the story line.

Since most introductory literature classes begin with study of the short story, it is here that you must establish a method for intelligent reading and writing about literature. The same essential principles apply to analysis of all types of literature, and the most basic one is to analyze and discuss the literature and not just recite its facts or story line. It may be helpful to distinguish between analysis and plot summary at this point.

Let us assume that you have been assigned a theme on the irony in Guy de Maupassant's short story "The Jewels." After carefully reading the story and marking instances of irony, you begin to write the first draft. If you merely present the plot details without shaping them or slanting them toward an interpretation, your theme might begin like this:

```
          Irony in "The Jewels"


     There is a lot of irony in "The Jewels," a

short story by Guy de Maupassant. The story is

about Monsieur Lantin, a provincial tax

collector who marries a young woman from a

poor but respectable family. Everyone thinks

highly of Lantin's wife. Before she married,

all who knew her kept repeating, "Happy will

be the man who wins her."
```

A similar opening paragraph, but one focusing upon irony, could be presented in this manner:

```
    Things aren't always what they seem. The

many ironies of "The Jewels," by Guy de

Maupassant, stem from the contrast between

Madame Lantin's virtuous reputation and her

lustful, materialistic nature. It is ironic

that Madame Lantin would take a lover because

she is, in outward appearances, the picture

of respectability. Those who chanted "Happy

will be the man who wins her" could not have

been more mistaken.
```

Both passages convey the information that a man named Lantin has married a woman with a good reputation. However, in order to stress the ironic contrast between reputation and reality in the second passage, the writer has jumped ahead in the story and presented the information that Madame Lantin later takes a lover. Notice also that the writer has used the key word "ironic." These are important differences. The second passage concentrates on the topic; the first passage is a mere rehash of details in the exact order in which they occur in the story.

This "jumping ahead" in an analysis paper is not only a means of focusing on the topic by bringing together pertinent related details, but it enables the writer to condense, or "telescope," the comments on the work of literature. Observing the limits of the topic, the analytical writer reshuffles the details of the selection being analyzed into the form that best conveys an interpretation—at the same time being careful not to distort the original sequence of events.

The best indication that rote plot summary reveals virtually nothing of importance about literature is the fact that you do not have to think in order to write it. A plot rehash indicates that you have read a piece of literature with your eyes, but not necessarily with your mind. An interpretive essay, on the other hand, expresses the mental connections a reader should make in order to understand the piece.

To illustrate, basically the same facts are presented in the two sample passages given above. The major difference is that the second (analytical) account indicates the critical writer's perception of how the author wanted his readers to react to the facts of his story (that is, to note the incongruity of Madame Lantin's reputation and her behavior). The first (plot summary) version merely presents isolated facts with no suggestion of how they should be interpreted in the context of the total story.

A second passage of plot summary might read as follows: "Lantin found only two faults in his wife: her love of the theater and her fondness for imitation jewelry." An analytical passage conveying the same information could be shaped like this:

```
Most of the irony is directed at Madame

Lantin's cuckolded husband. From the

beginning, Lantin objects to his wife's

fondness of the theater and "imitation"
```

jewelry. Lantin's concern is justified, but
not for the reasons he thinks: Madame
Lantin's frequent jaunts, supposedly to the
theater, make possible her affair with
another man, and her love of genuine jewelry
(not artificial, as her gullible husband
believes) causes her to turn to a man who can
give her the things her tax-collector husband
cannot. Adding to the irony is the fact that
poor Lantin considers his wife perfect except
for these two "frivolous" tastes.

Notice that the analytical passage is considerably
longer than the plot-summary version. If you have trouble
"thinking of something to write," you will find that the
problem disappears when you begin to focus on a controlling idea and explain and support your interpretations.

Following the story line, the next passage of plot
summary might read, "Madame Lantin returns shivering
from the opera one night and the next morning dies of
pneumonia. Monsieur Lantin is heartbroken."

Now an analysis of the same material, concentrating
upon irony: "The irony is heightened by the naiveté of the

wronged husband. So devoted is Lantin to his unfaithful wife that when she dies of pneumonia after a night at the 'opera,' he is so heartbroken that he 'almost followed her into the tomb.' " Although neither the word "irony" nor a synonym is used to ensure focus (too much such repetition is monotonous), notice that ironic incongruity is strongly implied by the adjective "unfaithful," which describes Madame Lantin and contrasts with the excessive grief of her wronged husband.

A typical plot rehash of Madame Lantin's death would go on to include the information that "after the death of his wife, Lantin is amazed that he cannot live alone on his pay as well as the two had lived previously." But an analysis would stress the ironic fact that the altered economy of the Lantin household inspires dumb amazement rather than suspicion in the still-unsuspecting cuckold.

When the hard-pressed Lantin is forced to sell his deceased wife's "baubles" and "eye-deceivers" in order to eat, he is astounded to learn that they are actually genuine and very valuable. An analysis should stress that the jewels are not "baubles," as the husband has believed, but they are indeed "eye-deceivers," though certainly not in the sense thought by Lantin. It is only his eyes which have been deceived by the jewels. Since Lantin's discovery of his wife's infidelity is the climax of the story, it is at this point that the controlling irony becomes evident: The jewels, which Lantin considered false and cheap, turn out to be genuine and exquisite, and his beautiful wife, whom he considered genuine and exquisite, turns out to be false and cheap.

Maupassant should have ended his story here, but he didn't. The plot summarizer, intent upon taking the story to its end, would write one last passage conveying the information that after selling the jewels, Lantin quits his job and, six months later (the author doesn't suggest why), marries a "respectable" second wife who "made him suffer a lot." Because the analytical writer has the benefit of selectivity, a critical paper need not mention this weak ending at all. If it is included in an interpretive paper, the writer could emphasize that the irony in this case is contrived and superfluous, a flaw in an otherwise well-written little story.

Comparison of the following two essays should help you see that analytical writing is far superior to plot summary.

Plot summary of "The Jewels"

Irony in "The Jewels"

There is a lot of irony in "The Jewels," a short story by Guy de Maupassant. The story is about Monsieur Lantin, a provincial tax collector who marries a young woman from a poor but respectable family. Everyone thinks highly of Lantin's wife. Before she married, all who knew her kept repeating, "Happy will be the man who wins her."

Lantin found only two faults in his wife:

her love of the theater and her fondness for imitation jewelry.

Madame Lantin returns shivering from the opera one night and the next morning dies of pneumonia. Monsieur Lantin is heartbroken. After the death of his wife, Lantin is amazed that he cannot live alone on his pay as well as the two had lived previously.

When Lantin is forced to sell his wife's jewels in order to eat, he learns that they are actually genuine and very valuable. He now knows his wife has been unfaithful.

He quits his job and, six months later, he marries a "respectable" second wife who "made him suffer a lot."

Analysis of "The Jewels"

Diamonds in the Rough

Things aren't always what they seem. The many ironies of "The Jewels," by Guy de

Maupassant, stem from the contrast between Madame Lantin's virtuous reputation and her lustful, materialistic nature. It is ironic that Madame Lantin would take a lover because she is, in outward appearances, the picture of respectability. Those who chanted "Happy will be the man who wins her" could not have been more mistaken.

Most of the irony is directed at Madame Lantin's cuckolded husband. From the beginning, Monsieur Lantin objects to his wife's fondness of the theater and "imitation" jewelry. Lantin's concern is justified, but not for the reasons he thinks: Madame Lantin's frequent jaunts, supposedly to the theater, make possible her affair with another man, and her love of genuine jewelry (not artificial, as her gullible husband believes) causes her to turn to a man who can give her the things her tax-collector husband cannot. Adding to the irony is the fact that

poor Lantin considers his wife perfect except
for these two "frivolous" tastes.

The irony is heightened by the naiveté of
the wronged husband. So devoted is Lantin to
his unfaithful wife that when she dies of
pneumonia after a night at the "opera," he is
so heartbroken that he "almost followed her
into the tomb." Oddly enough, he does not
become suspicious of Madame Lantin's
resources even when he finds that after her
death, "he cannot live alone on his pay as
well as the two had lived previously." That
two can live as cheaply as one is a romantic
stretching of economic probability, but it is
amazing that Lantin does not wonder how two
could live more cheaply than one.

Lantin's perhaps self—willed naiveté,
however, cannot withstand the hard facts of
his wife's life which are presented to him
when he is forced to sell her "baubles" and
"eye—deceivers" in order to eat. When he has

the jewels appraised, he is astounded to learn that they are actually genuine and very valuable. The jewels are not mere baubles, but they have in fact been eye-deceivers. The story reaches its delightfully ironic climax when Lantin learns that the jewels, which he thought false and cheap, are actually genuine and exquisite, and his beautiful wife, whom he believed genuine and exquisite, was actually false and cheap.

The story, which is tightly constructed to this point, is marred by the gratuitous irony of its conclusion. It would seem that the pathetic Lantin has suffered enough in his dealings with the fairer sex, but Maupassant has him marry a second "respectable" wife who also "made him suffer a lot." In spite of this forced ending, "The Jewels" is a brilliant piece of light fiction illustrating one of the many incongruities between appearance and reality.

The plot summary tells virtually nothing of significance about Maupassant's story. The analysis delves into its meaning and artistry by concentrating on the outstanding feature of irony. Also common in introductory literature classes are papers focusing on character or theme, as illustrated by the following sample essays.

Sample Essays

The Reluctant Realist
[Character-centered Analysis]

One of the things which makes literature interesting is characters that readers can relate to. Most readers probably can identify with the young narrator of Sherwood Anderson's "I Want to Know Why." He may be a bit extreme in his romanticism, but he is a typical adolescent in his naiveté and in his reluctance to face some hard facts of life.

The excessive romanticism of the narrator is illustrated by his passionate love of racehorses and racetracks. He says that

"Nothing smells better than coffee and manure and horses." Just being at a track gives him an emotional charge. In describing his feelings, he uses such glowing comments as "It's lovely" and "your heart thumps so you can hardly breathe." He romantically attributes idealized human qualities to thoroughbreds: "They're beautiful. There isn't anything so lovely and clean and full of spunk and honest." The boy's feeling for one horse, Sunstreak, is so strong that it makes him "ache to see him."

This intense romanticism is made possible, however, by the protagonist's naiveté about the less attractive side of racing—and of life. This innocence leads the boy to say that he can't see what gambling has to do with horses. Betting and shady characters have no place in his pure image of horseracing. He also idealizes the life of the black menials who work at the track and envies what he thinks is their carefree existence. When he and the trainer, Jerry Tillford, wordlessly communicate to each other their feeling that Sunstreak is special, the boy immediately assumes that Jerry is as pure and as innocent as he himself. He even says that he likes the trainer more than his own father because of their love of Sunstreak.

Such romantic naiveté is bound to be destroyed, and when it is, the boy shows a reluctance to face reality. When the narrator hears Jerry brag to a prostitute that it is he who deserves the credit for Sunstreak's victory, the boy, instead of admitting that he has overrated the trainer, hates Jerry for disappointing him. This hatred might be lessened if the boy realized his own awakening sexuality, indicated by his long look

at the prostitutes through the farmhouse
window, but he can't face the fact that he may
share some of the trainer's human "weakness."
Instead of modifying his unrealistic view of
life in light of this disillusioning experience, the boy merely says that he "can't make
it out." As the story ends, he is still
blaming Jerry and not his unrealistic expectations for the fact that "At the tracks the
air don't taste as good or smell as good" as
it used to. It probably never will.

The protagonist's reluctance to give up
the comfortable world of childhood for a
world which is less than perfect is under-
standable. But facing such a world and then
establishing a reasonable sense of its good
and its bad is part of growing up. In both his
youthful optimism and his deep disappoint-
ment when his naive view of life is shattered,
the boy represents universal human traits.

A Race With Time
[Theme-centered Analysis]

Maturing is a gradual process, but
sometimes an especially important event
speeds it along. Sherwood Anderson's "I Want
to Know Why" recounts such an experience,
during which the fifteen-year-old narrator
painfully loses his innocence and is ini-
tiated into the real world he will have to
cope with as an adult. The story's theme is
that such disillusionment is a necessary and
inevitable part of growing up.

To set up this transformation, Anderson
first establishes the romantic naiveté of the
young narrator. Racetracks and horses are
especially thrilling to him. The boy's
romanticism is evident in his statement that
"Nothing smells better than coffee and manure
and horses." When he's at a racetrack, his
"heart thumps" so that he can "hardly
breathe." The boy even believes he can tell

which horse is going to win by the way he feels when he looks at it. He considers Sunstreak special because "It makes you ache to see him," another indication that he is governed by intensely romantic emotions.

The boy also idealizes the people associated with racetracks. Preferring not to face the shady side of racing, he says that he can't see what gamblers like his friend's father have to do with horses. He naively believes the blacks who do the dirty work at the track are better off than he, and he envies what he thinks is their carefree existence. His special romantic idol, however, is Jerry Tillford, Sunstreak's trainer. The boy believes that Jerry shares his own mystical feelings about the horse and, to an extent, the trainer does. After Jerry and the narrator wordlessly communicate to each other their mutual appreciation of Sunstreak, he says that he likes Jerry even more than he ever liked his own father. This statement reflects a hero worship typical of immature youth.

Like all people in the real world, however, Jerry Tillford has human flaws, and this realization leads to the young boy's disillusionment. His dreamworld crumbles after the race when he hears the trainer bragging to a prostitute that it is he who deserves the credit for Sunstreak's victory. Hurt and disillusioned, the boy hates Jerry as impulsively as he had loved him a short time before. Although the disenchanted youth probably doesn't realize it, part of his anger is disgust and guilt over his own awakening sexual impulses. He looks long and hard at the prostitutes through the farmhouse window, and he remembers them in vivid detail. He even compares one of them to his beloved Sunstreak.

"I Want to Know Why" illustrates that

humans--the young narrator included--aren't always as "lovely and clean and . . . honest as some racehorses." Because of this new insight into life, "the air don't taste as good or smell as good" to the boy as it did in his days of innocence. At the end of the story, he is bewildered by this change, but when he's a little older, he'll understand that his disillusionment was just a matter of time, a part of growing up.

Rock of Ages

In "A Visit of Charity," Eudora Welty satirizes a purely social concept of charity. In Welty's "A Worn Path," Phoenix Jackson, an ancient black woman, personifies the Christian love which inspires true charity. Her courageous, reverent, and unselfish journey symbolizes life lived righteously, and her name suggests that those who make the

pilgrimage in the spirit of Phoenix are the
only victors over death. Like the mythical
phoenix, they will be constantly renewed,
spiritually born again out of their own
ashes.

This theme is developed primarily by
symbolism. Phoenix's journey is depicted as a
ritual representing the spiritual way the old
woman has lived her life. Though her eyes are
"blue with age," she sets out on her treacherous mission into town with unwavering confidence and dedication, looking "straight
ahead" and marching "like a festival figure
in some parade." Such description emphasizes
Phoenix's dignity and the importance of her
journey.

To complete this quest, Phoenix must
overcome many obstacles. The natural
hindrances she does not fear; in fact, she
seems to welcome them as fellow participants
in the ceremony of life. When a thornbush

snags her dress, she says, "Thorns, you doing
your appointed work." That Phoenix is in tune
with life's timeless rhythms is suggested by
her relationship to nature. Making her way
through the "quivering" underbrush, she
recites a litany to the animal world: "Out of
my way, all you foxes, owls, beetles, jack
rabbits, coons and wild animals! . . . Keep
out from under these feet, little bob-whites.
. . . Keep the big wild hogs out of my path."
Her journey is eased by small favors from
Nature and God: "Glad this not the season for
bulls . . . , and the good Lord made his snakes
to crawl up and sleep in the winter," says
Phoenix.

Life is such a joyous mystery to Phoenix
that she doesn't fear even the supernatural.
"A pleasure I don't see no two-headed snake
coming around that tree, where it come once,"
she mumbles to herself. "It took a while to
get by him, back in the summer." When she

mistakes a scarecrow for a ghost, she addresses it quite naturally: "'Ghost,' she said sharply, 'who be you the ghost of?'"

Neither the natural nor the supernatural presents a real threat to Phoenix. Man-made obstacles, however, are a different matter. When Phoenix encounters a foot-log spanning a creek, she says, "Now comes the trial." She triumphs by trusting, closing her eyes, and crossing. Then a barbed-wire fence forces her to abandon her "festival figure" dignity and "creep and crawl . . . like a baby." By so humbling herself, she passes this test.

As Phoenix draws near the town, she encounters her real adversary: the material-istic, "civilized" world represented by the hunter. Faced with this more formidable threat, Phoenix becomes vulnerable. When she attempts to chase his black dog from her path, she tumbles into a ditch and cannot regain her feet. However, nature again provides for

Phoenix, as some "old dead weeds" break her
fall. Phoenix is not hurt, but she is at the
mercy of the hunter, who addresses her
condescendingly as "Granny" and assumes that
she is going into town to see Santa Claus. The
hunter's relationship to nature is in marked
contrast to Phoenix's. Explaining his trip
from town, he says, "I get something for my
trouble," then pats a stuffed game bag from
which hangs "a little closed claw." Moments
before, spying quail "walking around like
pullets," Phoenix has said "Walk pretty." The
hunter uses life selfishly; Phoenix
celebrates it.

But Phoenix, no doubt through long
practice, knows how to deal with the hunter.
She tricks him into childishly chasing a
stray dog so that she can retrieve a nickel
she has seen fall from his pocket. The hunter
is the strongest threat yet encountered, but
Phoenix does not fear him. When he returns

from his chase and cruelly points his gun at her, Phoenix says, "I seen plenty go off closer by, in my day." Phoenix's harsh judgment of herself for taking the coin ("God watching me the whole time. I come to stealing.") is lightened when the hunter lies, "I'd give you a dime if I had any money with me." Her "stealing" is totally excused, as is her begging, when she later uses the money to buy her hopelessly ill grandson a small Christmas gift. Even Phoenix's "wrongs" are right.

The hunter, a corrupt intruder into Phoenix's pure world of nature, foreshadows the second part of the story. When Phoenix finally arrives in the "paved city," the colors of the Natchez Trace are replaced by the artificial gaiety of "red and green electric lights" and "red-, green-, and silver-wrapped" Christmas packages. Here Phoenix must cope with the spiritual relatives of the hunter. With solemn dignity, she allows a lady shopper, who addresses her as "Grandma," to tie her shoe. When she enters the doctor's office to get the medicine for her grandson, Phoenix is subjected to insults. She is again addressed as "Grandma" by an attendant who says "A charity case, I suppose." A nurse enters and says "Oh, that's just old Phoenix," but then adds, with a significance beyond her understanding, "She doesn't come for herself." Through all this abuse, Phoenix maintains a "stiff and ceremonial dignity," sitting "bolt upright" in her chair. When Phoenix's mission is finally accomplished and the nurse marks down "Charity" in her ledger, the difference between socialized charity and charity of the heart is emphasized.

It is significant that "A Worn Path" takes place at Christmas, when the spiritual values of Christ supposedly are commemorated and

celebrated. Of all the characters in the
story, only Phoenix lives by these values.
Phoenix's goodness is natural and instinctive. She is, in the deepest sense, in tune
with nature—her own and life's. When Phoenix
says of her sick grandson, "He suffer and it
don't seem to put him back at all. He got a
sweet look. He going to last," the statement
is also Welty's tribute to Phoenix and the
rare virtues she represents.

POETRY ANALYSIS

Poetry analysis presents special problems because
poets communicate meaning in varied and subtle ways.
Before you can write a worthwhile analysis of a poem, you
must of course understand it. Before you can begin to understand a poem, you must identify the type of poem you
are dealing with.

Whether a short story is written from first or third-
person point of view is an important key to its meaning.
The same is true of poetry. It is essential, for instance, that
the critical writer recognize that "My Last Duchess," the
subject of the sample essay "Will There Be Another?," is a
dramatic monologue. The poem presents a little "drama"
with a speaker and an audience. As in a first-person short
story, the words of the poem are spoken by a character and
not by the author. The poet may not agree with the

speaker's viewpoint. Therefore, to credit the duke's statements to Browning would be to misread the poem. That
the duke's opinion of his wife is distorted by his ego is the
key which unlocks its underlying ironic meaning.

The essay "Scornful Child" is an analysis of another
character-portrait poem, but unlike "My Last Duchess,"
"Miniver Cheevy" is written from a third-person point of
view and does not have a dramatic situation. Like "My
Last Duchess," it is an ironic poem, but the irony stems
from the *author's* choice of words, not Cheevy's. In analyzing "Miniver Cheevy," therefore, you would state "Robinson says" or "the poet says." In writing about "My Last
Duchess," you would state "the duke says" or "the
speaker says."

"The Mill," the subject of the essay "Where Have All
the Flowers Gone?," is yet another type of poem. Like
"Miniver Cheevy," it is narrated from a third-person point
of view; but unlike "Miniver Cheevy," it tells a story. Like
"My Last Duchess," it is a dramatic poem; but unlike "My
Last Duchess," it is dramatic in the sense that it depicts
overt action rather than static situation. Such poems are
called "narrative," and they resemble both fiction and
drama. Narrative poems are characterized by plot, "ac-
tors," and sometimes even dialogue, and they communicate meaning through the interaction of character and
events, colored, of course, by language.

"Hap," the subject of the essay "Due to Circumstances Beyond Our Control . . . ," calls for still
another critical approach. The poem is a straightforward
presentation of a philosophical concept. Its meaning is
communicated directly by the poet, not through a character, situation, or action. The absence of these dramatic devices suggests that the thoughts of the poem are those of
the poet himself—that the author, Thomas Hardy, is not

communicating *a* point of view, but *his* point of view. Analysis of such a poem will concentrate upon tone, imagery, and even direct statement (which is rare in other kinds of poems). A similar type of poem, but one in which the author communicates an emotion more than an idea, is called "lyrical." Because philosophical and lyrical poems are so much alike, they require essentially the same critical approach. In the absence of character and plot, the analytical writer must concentrate even more than usual on the connotations of the language of these poems.

Sample Essays

Will There Be Another?

The way a person tells a story often is more interesting—and more revealing—than the story itself. Such is the case of Robert Browning's famous poem "My Last Duchess." The duke's self-serving account of the demise of his last wife tells the count's envoy—and the reader—much more about the Duke of Ferrara than it does about the woman he thinks has wronged him. The poem is filled with

irony. In attempting to justify his treatment
of his last duchess, the duke, by his own
words, probably ruins his chances of
contracting a new marriage which he greatly
desires.

The poem is a perfect union of form and
content. It is a dramatic monologue written
in iambic pentameter couplets, a form which
is consistent with the serious business the
duke is attempting to conduct just beneath
the strained informality of his conversation.
The lines rhyme in pairs throughout the
fifty-six-line poem, but the rhymes are so
smooth that they are hardly noticed.
Moreover, Browning has taken pains to
construct the duke's speech so as to avoid the
metronome effect of end-stopped couplets.
Amazingly, there are only two end-stopped
rhymes in the entire monologue, and one of
these is the last line of the poem. To offset
these end-stopped rhymes, Browning has

employed slant rhyme in both of them
("whate'er"--"everywhere" and "rarity"--
"me"). By using slant rhymes and enjamb-
ment (carrying a rhyming line over into the
next line), Browning has constructed the
poem to suggest just the right mood of loose
formality and also to hint at the duke's
wiliness. The speech the duke delivers to the
count's messenger probably is one he has
spoken to visitors before or possibly even
rehearsed as his pitch for the count's
daughter. He is a stiff and formal man, much
given to protocol, but in this important
speech which is thinly disguised as casual
conversation, he wishes to appear relaxed and
natural. He doesn't quite make it.

The poem begins in medias res, with the
duke pointing out to the count's envoy the
picture of his last duchess, "Looking as if
she were alive." The duke, seemingly without
knowing it, reveals his insensitivity and

egotism from the very first. Although the woman apparently is now dead by the duke's orders ("I gave commands; / Then all smiles stopped together"), he still values the response which her beauty, captured in the painting, can evoke from others. Consistent with his attitude toward the woman when she was alive, the duke discusses her as he would an art object, a possession. As the duke's words soon reveal, the lady's failure to fulfill that role—and that role alone—led to her death.

The duke's dissatisfaction with his late wife seems to have resulted from the conflict between her natural, innocent joy in living and the stern duke's "nine-hundred-years-old name." It is pathetically ironic that the duke never mentioned his unhappiness to his bride because "E'en then would be some stooping; and I choose / Never to stoop." The duke could not forgive his wife for not

sharing his pride in his position. "She had / A
heart," says the duke, "too soon made glad."
The duchess seems to have had no sense of
social superiority, a dangerously liberal
attitude for one married to a man obsessed
with his birth and position:

> Sir, 'twas all one! My favor at
>   her breast,
> The drooping of the daylight in
>   the West,
> The bough of cherries some
>   officious fool
> Broke in the orchard for her.

The duke is so blinded by egotism that he
blames his last duchess for not ranking his
favors above the sunset! The love that the
duke's servants had for the lady is signified
by the gift of a bough of cherries, just as

the duke's contempt for all underlings is
suggested by his epithet "some officious
fool."

All of this probably is not wasted on the
envoy. The importance of his mission, to
contract a marriage for his master's
daughter, marks him as a shrewd and trusted
ambassador. The envoy, like the reader, forms
an impression of the duke's character based
upon the duke's own words. Surely the count's
representative will warn his master against
making the dangerous match which the duke
proposes. At the end of the poem there is
perhaps a hint of the envoy's opinion of the
duke, who desires the rich dowry which would
accompany such a marriage. The duke's avarice
gets the better of him in his final pitch for
the count's daughter. His greed is only
thinly veiled by his hypocritical statement
that his real desire is for the woman herself:

> The Count your master's known
>   munificence
> Is ample warrant that no just
>   pretence
> Of mine for dowry will be
>   disallowed;
> Though his fair daughter's self, as
>   I avowed
> At starting, is my object.

If the envoy has not yet been convinced, the duke's sliding into the slick language of high diplomacy after earlier contending "Even had you skill / In speech——which I have not" should persuade the agent of the count that he is dealing with a dangerous adversary indeed.

The envoy never speaks in the poem, but immediately following this last bit of business we hear the duke say, "Nay, we'll go / Together down, sir." At this point, the count's ambassador probably knows all he

needs to know about the duke. The duke's
protest suggests that the envoy has begun to
take his leave. Under normal circumstances,
an ambassador would never initiate the ending
of a meeting with a nobleman. At this stage of
the negotiations, however, the envoy may not
be thinking of protocol but of escaping this
viperous man.

In a final note of irony, the duke,
apparently still unaware of the impression he
has made, can't resist directing his
visitor's attention to another art object.
His command to "Notice Neptune, though, /
Taming a sea-horse" brings the poem full
circle, and the sculpture serves as a fitting
image of the relationship between the duke
and his last duchess: It depicts an
all-powerful god mastering a beautiful,
natural creature.

In this great poem, Robert Browning has
perfectly blended form and content to achieve

an ironic self-revelation of character. The poet's sympathies obviously are with the late duchess as the brutal duke engages in a speech which is virtually self-satire. In "My Last Duchess," Browning indirectly praises the natural and damns narrow, dehumanizing convention. The duchess is destroyed, but the duke receives poetic justice.

Scornful Child

E. A. Robinson is noted for his character portraits, and "Miniver Cheevy" is among his more devastating ones. Miniver Cheevy is satirically portrayed as a man who blames his unhappiness on the world into which he was born. Robinson's sarcastic tone, however, makes it clear that the real cause of Miniver's failure is his own weakness of character.

Miniver Cheevy is a natural pessimist, a

born grumbler. His hatred of life is so great that he even "assailed the seasons." The double meaning of "He wept that he was ever born, / And he had reasons" is directed at Cheevy: Literally, the statement identifies Miniver as the type of person who is all too willing to pour out his hard-luck story, but it also implies that such a person _does_ have valid reasons for mourning his miserable life. He, of course, won't admit these.

Miniver likes to think he would have been a great success had he been born in "days of old." "Miniver sighed for what was not" implies that the romanticized times he longs for never really existed, that Cheevy's world is no better nor worse than the world humanity has always had to contend with. Miniver Cheevy, with his petty spirit, would be out of tune with _any_ period of history, and especially with the supposedly heroic days of Thebes and Camelot. In fact, if Miniver's own time is especially shabby and materialistic, then it is the perfect time for him to live. His vision of bright swords, prancing steeds, and bold warriors contrasts humorously with the image of a dancing Miniver Cheevy. He mourns the modern decline of art and romance, but his own "labors" consist only of sighing and dreaming. That Cheevy's concept of the past is superficial, escapist, and self-serving is indicated by the fact that could he have been a Medici, he would have used his opportunities not in a creative way but merely as a license to sin. Miniver's vision of the present is so warped by his distortion of the past that he loathes even the functional khaki of the modern soldier and misses "the medieval grace / Of iron clothing," or armor.

Just as Cheevy rejects his own culture because he cannot find a place in it, so does he scorn its gold—not for the shallow materialism it symbolizes, but simply because he is "annoyed . . . without it." Petty, selfish values and not high ideals again motivate Miniver's condemnation of the modern world. That Cheevy is too morally weak to act upon his dissatisfaction is emphasized by the sarcastic repetition of "Miniver thought, and thought, and thought, / And thought about it."

The concluding quatrain finds Cheevy still thinking, coughing and calling it fate, and indulging in yet another form of escapism, drinking. When Robinson says that Cheevy was "born too late," he not only sums up Miniver's evaluation of his plight but implies a judgment of his own: Since the Miniver Cheevys of the world, no matter when they live, consider themselves born too late into cultures unappreciative of their talents, it would be better if they were never born at all.

"Miniver Cheevy" is one of Robinson's most

devastating character portraits. Unlike the
author's noble failures, Cheevy is not the
victim of external forces over which he has no
control. Neither is it contradictory that
Robinson personally shared Cheevy's distaste
for the modern world. He does not satirize
Miniver's condemnation of modern culture so
much as the envy and self-pity which motivate
it. In fact, Miniver Cheevy, the self-serving
loser who blames all his ills on society, is a
contemporary stereotype.

Where Have All the Flowers Gone?

Many of E. A. Robinson's poems warn
against the dehumanizing effects of
materialism. In "The Mill," a brief narrative
poem, the villain is technology, materialism's servant. The poem, dated 1920, depicts
the human tragedy which can result when a
person is deprived of the dignity of labor.

The tone is bleak. The poem opens with a
picture of the miller's wife, who "had waited
long" for her husband's return. The images of
the cold tea and dead fire foreshadow her
later discovery, when she seeks out her tardy
husband, of his corpse "hanging from a beam"
in the deserted mill. She should have known
something was amiss when the miller "lingered
at the door," as if to say a final good-bye.
His parting remark, "There are no millers any
more" both hints at his suicide and gives the
reason for it.

The miller's wife soon shares her
husband's grim view of life. The world has
passed the miller by. He falls pathetic
victim to a culture in which most of the work
that people once took pride in is now done
impersonally by machines. This same sense of
displacement engulfs the miller's wife when
she enters the mill, where there lingers "a
warm / And mealy fragrance of the past," a

sense of well-being now forever gone. Fleeing
the grotesque corpse hanging from a beam, she
"may have reasoned," says the narrator, that
there was only one escape from her overwhelming despair. She chooses death by
drowning in the millpond, "one way of the few
there were" which would "hide her and would
leave no mark." The desire of the miller's
wife for an obscure death is especially
pitiful because the despair of both the
miller and his wife has resulted from their
being deprived of the opportunity to leave
their mark in life. They are anachronisms
from a time when people derived much of their
identity and sense of worth from dignified
labor. The modern world has no place for the
miller or his wife.

At this point in the narrative there is a
remarkable shift in tone as the imagery
becomes romantically somber. The miller's
wife, in her new circumstances, views death

as a serene escape from a brutal world. The millpond, soon to be her grave, is described as "Black water, smooth above the weir / Like starry velvet in the night." This, the narrator implies, is how the water must have looked to the defeated woman in her final, tranquil moment of decision.

The poem, however, ends on a note of stark realism. The pond, "Though ruffled once" by the woman's plunging body, "would soon appear/ The same as ever to the sight." This statement serves as a perfect epitaph for the miller and his wife. Their existence has briefly ruffled the surface of life, but because they have outlived their usefulness, they die and leave no mark. They will not be missed.

Robinson, of course, hoped that his readers would not be unruffled by this tragic story. Despite the surface objectivity of the account, the poet's sympathies obviously are

with the "little people" who cannot survive
in an impersonal, mechanized world.

Due to Circumstances Beyond Our Control . . .

"Philosophical" poems, or poems designed
to communicate a fundamental belief in a
straightforward manner, are rare because
poets usually present their ideas indirectly
through characterization, dramatic
situation, or a combination of the two.
Thomas Hardy's "Hap," however, directly
states an idea. The absence of a dramatic
situation and of a dramatic character, or
persona, suggests that Hardy intended the
poem simply as a statement of his own personal
view of the indifferent workings of fate.

In the first eight lines of the sonnet,
Hardy states a hypothetical proposition. He
says that if some vengeful god sent him his

suffering and enjoyed his sorrow, "Then would I bear it, clench myself, and die." Then he would at least have the consolation of being the wronged innocent, victim of divine "ire unmerited." Ironically, suffering under such circumstances would also prove a godhead, "a Powerfuller than I," the existence of which would provide at least a "Half-eased mind."

"But," as Hardy writes at the beginning of line nine, it is "not so." The last six lines of the poem comment on the problem stated in the first eight. The transitional "But not so," which denies the possibility of the proposition stated in the first part of the poem, is followed by a rhetorical question, expressed somewhat awkwardly in Hardy's inimitable language: "How arrives it joy lies slain, / And why unblooms the best hope ever sown?"—how does it happen that our joy is destroyed and why are our hopes not permitted to bloom into fruition?

Hardy's answer is that there is no logical or comforting answer. Human affairs proceed not according to divine law, cruel or otherwise, but by mere chance. "Crass Casualty obstructs" the nurturing elements of "sun and rain," and Time is but a gambler randomly casting the dice of joy and sadness. The "Powerfuller" is not only a "Doomster" but a "purblind," or completely blind, Doomster. Hardy's complaint to the gods which do not exist is not that we suffer but that our suffering is the result of pure chance, and therefore without meaning. This haphazard nature of life robs even joy of significance because fate "had as readily strown / Blisses about my pilgrimage as pain." Happiness is just as purposeless as sorrow.

"Hap" projects a grim picture of the universe. Life is controlled by neither mortal nor God. Bliss and pain fall at random. Hardy's system rejects not only the possibility of a benevolent God but of a cruel one as well. The ruling spirit of the world, Hardy concludes, is the indifferent God of Chance, which is a way of saying that there is no order, only chaos.

NOVEL ANALYSIS

The critical principles for analyzing novels are essentially the same as those for short stories. The main difference between the two forms is that the novel has a much broader range than the short story, enabling novelists to present subplots and many characters and to develop their themes more deliberately. Yet the two genres are cut from the same cloth and, in fact, merge in the novelette, which may be regarded as either a long short story or a short novel.

In analyzing a novel, you must adjust your critical method in order to account for the larger scale of the genre. Especially in writing a short paper, you must be scrupulously selective by employing either one of two approaches: telescoping or microscoping. Selectivity by *telescoping* is achieved by the overview, in which you comment on the most significant aspects of the entire book. "Delivered from Evil" exemplifies such an essay. Selectivity by *microscoping* is achieved by isolating one particular characteristic for close examination instead of commenting on the total effect of the book. "Reflections Upon a Golden Eye" is an example of this type of essay.

In an overview, you scan the landscape with binoculars and present a panoramic view. In a microscopic essay, you examine a single feature through a magnifying glass.

Sample Essays

Delivered from Evil

James Dickey's <u>Deliverance</u> gives a new dimension to the cliché that people, for all their civilized veneer, are still savages. Ed, the narrator and protagonist, is reborn through the experience of a primeval struggle with the elements and with mountain men as treacherous as the winding river which serves as the setting for this exciting novel.

The four men who challenge the wild backwoods of north Georgia are typical middle-class Americans. It is due mainly to the prodding of Lewis, a macho physical-fitness fanatic, that the other three go at all. Early in the book, Lewis foreshadows the harrowing test of Ed's manhood with the statement that survival "came down to the man, and what he could do. The body is the one thing you can't fake; it's just got to be there." This pronouncement seems melodramatic to the other three men, who would rather play golf than go off on a canoe trip. "Ah, he's going to turn this into something," Ed scoffs to himself. "A life principle. A Way." Lewis' statement, however, proves prophetic. Before the journey is completed, its truth is experienced by all four men, each in his own way.

Of the four, Ed is the deepest and most sensitive. He also is the most bored with life. Lewis has his survival games; Bobby, a "surface human being," has his shallow cynicism; Drew has his family and his job——he keeps a copy of the company history on his coffee table. Ed has only the existential emptiness of the "feeling of the incon-sequence of whatever I would do." Vice-president of a small advertising agency, he finds his work neither challenging nor

fulfilling. Just how dull his marriage has
become is emphasized by the fact that during
intercourse with his wife before leaving on
the trip, he thinks of an advertising model he
met the day before, an ordinary enough girl
but one in whose eyes the hungry Ed had
searched for "another life, deliverance."
The four men gather for the trip,
appropriately, at a new shopping center.

That the suburbanites are about to enter
into another world is suggested by the odd
characters they meet at the edge of the
wilderness: the inbred albino banjo-picker
and the hulking Griner brothers, who are
hired to drive the cars to the pickup point.
But nothing could prepare them for the
creatures they are soon to encounter. The
first day on the river is idyllic, as Lewis
introduces his companions to the exhilarating
dangers of white water. Early the second day,
however, there occurs an event so grotesquely

horrifying that their wildest imaginings
could not have prepared them for it. When Ed
and Bobby are separated from the others, they
fall into the clutches of a pair of shotgun-
toting mountaineers. Ed is tied to a tree;
then one of the men sodomizes the pathetic
Bobby. The almost palpable horror of the
scene culminates when the hidden Lewis drives
an arrow through this monster. The other man,
who had been preparing to sodomize Ed,
manages to escape in the confusion. Before
being rescued by Lewis, Ed had experienced a
tentative grace under pressure when he coolly
contemplated his own death and wondered what
the barrel openings of the shotgun held at his
chest would look like "at the exact instant
they went off." But this may have been more
shock than courage. Ed had obediently dropped
to his knees when the mountain men demanded
it.

From this moment, the novel is one of

almost unbearable suspense as the weekend
adventurers both pursue and flee the
surviving backwoodsman as they struggle down
the river toward civilization. The canoes
wreck and Drew is killed, either by the
mountain man's bullet or by bashing his head
against a rock. Lewis thinks he saw Drew
flinch from a bullet before capsizing into
the roaring current, but the other two aren't
sure, a fact which adds to the suspense. Is
the mountaineer really stalking them on the
high cliffs bordering the river or is he just
a phantom of their heightened imaginations?
Because Lewis has broken his leg in the wreck,
the burden—and the challenge—of leadership
falls to Ed. Running the river, originally a
mere sporting test of endurance, is now a
matter of life and death. The very survival
of the three men depends upon what Ed is
made of.

When Ed takes charge, a transformation

begins. Drawing upon an untapped reservoir of strength and courage, he climbs the sheer cliff in darkness, lays an ambush for the mountain man, and the next morning coldly kills him with his primitive weapon, a bow and arrow. The change in Ed is signified by the fact that on the first morning of the trip he had missed a deer because of a last-second failure of nerve. But now the game has changed to a primeval contest of kill-or-be-killed, and the only law is survival of the fittest.

It is a game that Ed quickly learns to enjoy. While he is stalking his prey and during and after the kill, Ed has never felt so alive, so much in tune with himself. This second Ed is so far removed from his civilized counterpart that he even finds pleasure in the wound inflicted by his own arrow when he tumbles from his tree ambush. "There had never been a freedom like it. The pain itself was freedom, and the blood," Ed thinks, as he cuts the arrow from his side. So alien are the laws of civilization that it little matters to Ed that the man he has killed may not be the right one. At the time Ed released the arrow, he thought its target was his mortal enemy. Ed has vanquished his adversary, whether he is real or surrogate. Either way, he has faced his moment of truth without flinching. Guilt and compunction belong to that other world which Ed has so easily shucked off.

The "After" section of the book makes it clear that what Ed has learned about himself (and, Dickey implies, about the true nature of humans) will be carried back to that other world. "The river and everything I remembered about it became a possession to me, a personal, private possession, as nothing else in my life ever had. Now it ran nowhere but in my head, but there it ran as though immortally," Ed tells the reader. He returns to the humdrum of family and job and, if anything, even begins to appreciate their tameness a bit. He can now afford to, sustained as he is by the secret knowledge that just beneath his dull, ordinary exterior there lurks a gloriously primitive, elementally brave, delivered spirit.

Reflections Upon a Golden Eye

James Dickey's <u>Deliverance</u> makes exciting escape reading, in both senses of the term. So mesmerizing is the suspense of the river journey, in fact, that most readers probably overlook Dickey's inconsistent handling of one of the novel's recurrent symbols, the gold spot in the eye of the Kitt'n Britches model.

This symbol is introduced early, in the "Before" section of the book: "There was a peculiar spot, a kind of tan slice, in her left eye, and it hit me with, I knew right away, strong powers." A few pages later, Ed, the narrator, recalls the image of the golden eye during a somewhat mechanical act of intercourse with his wife:

> It was the heat of another person around me, the moving heat, that brought the image up. The girl from the studio threw back her hair and clasped her breast, and in the center of Martha's heaving and expertly working back, the gold eye shone, not with the practicality of sex, so necessary to its survival, but the promise of it that promised other things, another life, deliverance.

Obviously, much of the philosophic weight of the novel rests upon this symbol, mentioned

as closely as it is in conjunction with the
allusion to the book's title. Here, the
golden eye seems to represent excitement and
adventure, a realm of mysterious potential
entirely unlike the dull routine of Ed's
life, which has given him a "feeling of the
inconsequence of whatever I would do." It is
therefore all the more surprising that when
Ed _is_ delivered into the primitive world of
the river, where the consequence of his
action will be his very survival, he searches
for, but fails to find, his "slice of gold":
"I looked for a slice of gold like the model's
in the river: some kind of freckle, something
lovable, in the huge serpent-shape of light."
The symbol seems now to have shifted to
represent something akin to domestic security, not deliverance from it. The golden eye
is likened to the tame and the ordinary: "some
kind of freckle, something lovable." Yet the

slice of gold is still described as "like the
model's," earlier equated with "deliverance." Inexplicably, the symbol now
represents both the ordinary and its
mysterious opposite.

Dickey returns again to the symbol of the
eye in the "After" section as a means, it
would seem, of tying things together. Ed has
survived his ordeal, has in fact proved
himself a hero of sorts, and is now
philosophizing about his experience:

> Because of the associations she had
> for me, I looked up the girl in the
> Kitt'n Britches ad and took her out
> to dinner a couple of times. I still
> loved the way she looked, but her
> gold-halved eye had lost its
> fascination. Its place was in the
> night river, in the land of

impossibility. That's where its magic was for me. I left it there, though I would have liked to see her hold her breast once more, in a small space full of men. I see her every now and then, and the studio uses her. She is a pleasant part of the world, but minor. She is imaginary.

This passage makes the symbol all the more confusing. The girl and the symbol are merged, and both are dismissed by Ed as "minor" and "imaginary." But if the place of the "gold-halved eye" is "in the night river, in the land of impossibility," a land which Ed has found all too possible and which has changed his very being, then how can the experience ever be to Ed only a minor and imaginary part of his world? Such a pat dismissal suggests that Dickey has confused his symbol with the model it is associated with—a character who is indeed so unrealized as to be almost imaginary. It may be that the model is simply too ordinary to carry the weight of this important symbol.

<u>Deliverance</u> is a spellbinding, nearly perfect adventure story. It would be an even sounder novel had Dickey forgone Ed's muddled reflections upon the model's golden eye.

DRAMA ANALYSIS

The student writer in an introductory literature course may analyze drama without any specialized knowledge of how drama differs from other literary genres. There are, in fact, several basic similarities. As in most fiction and some forms of poetry, the meaning of a play evolves through action, and the people are characterized by what they say and do. With rare exception, there is no place in drama for author comment, or exposition, but most fiction writers and poets also communicate their meaning dramatically and indirectly. The dramatist, compared to writers in other genres, has to do even more showing than telling, but this is a difference of degree more than kind.

In brief, drama may be analyzed in much the same way that you analyze fiction and dramatic poetry, as the following overview of Edward Albee's *The Sandbox* illustrates.

Sample Essay

Boxed In

Many contemporary writers are depicting Americans as others might see us. Edward Albee is such a writer. In The Sandbox, his little absurdist masterpiece, Albee satirizes our shallow values, our phoniness, and our loss of humanity.

Mommy and Daddy represent typical American middle-class adults. The fact that they address each other by title and not by name serves a double purpose. "Mommy" and "Daddy" are terms of phony endearment, as well as universalizing labels. The marriage is without affection, and the couple is devoid of individual humanizing traits. Daddy

is the stereotyped henpecked husband
("Whatever you say, Mommy"); Mommy is the
stereotyped domineering woman ("Well, of
course . . . whatever I say"). Their cold,
sterile relationship both defines the
characters' emptiness and suggests the
emotional bankruptcy which characterizes
many modern marriages. The ties that bind
Mommy and Daddy are merely legal and sickly
symbiotic; there is no bond of love.

Loveless marriage sets the tone of the
play, but the primary target of Albee's
social satire is America's treatment of the
aged. Mommy and Daddy, Mr. and Mrs. Middle
America, have brought Grandma, who is
actually Mommy's mommy and apparently not a
grandma at all, to the beach to die. In the
surrealistic staging of the play, the beach
is represented by a child's sandbox, which
also symbolizes America's tendency to treat
the aged as if they were mental children.

Mommy and Daddy tote Grandma onstage, "their hands under her armpits; she is quite rigid; her legs are drawn up, her feet do not touch the ground." Handling her as if she were a piece of outdated furniture, or worse, they "dump her" in the sandbox. Grandma's response to such treatment is somewhere between "a baby's laugh and cry." Her "Graaaaa" also resembles the growling of an animal, suggesting the degree to which the old woman has been brutalized.

This animal imagery is picked up again later in the play when Grandma pathetically likens herself to an underfoot pet: "They . . . fixed a nice place for me under the stove . . . gave me an army blanket . . . and my own dish . . . my very own dish!" This implied comparison to a pet cat takes on an even more brutal meaning when Grandma, to signify the acceptance of her death, busily shovels sand over herself. In this, the strongest image of the play, the old woman buries herself like so much excrement in the sandbox, which has now become a litter box. Grandma understates the obvious when she says, "There's no respect around here!" The truly pathetic thing, however, is that the old lady has been deprived even of her self-respect.

Albee implies that this cruel treatment of the aged is the logical result of our youth worship. Youth worship, in turn, is the result of our plastic, materialistic cultural values. Appropriately enough, the Angel of Death is a "good-looking, well-built boy in a bathing suit," a product of Southern California, the source of many of our contemporary social mores. He has no identity apart from his youth and beautiful body because the studio hasn't given him one yet. Aside from poor delivery of a couple of rehearsed lines, his only function in the play is to do calisthenics and deliver the

kiss of death. This Angel of the Body
Beautiful represents our national obsession
with the purely physical, the appearance and
not the substance of things. Sadly, even
Grandma, who suffers most from the shallow
values symbolized by this plastic character,
is so brainwashed by our fleshly national
philosophy that when the Young Man flexes his
muscles, she marvels, "Isn't that something?"
Pitifully courting youth, when the Angel
delivers the kiss of death, Grandma says,
"You did that very well, dear."

Stereotyped emotional hypocrites to the
end, Mommy and Daddy respond to Grandma's
death with all the appropriate clichés. "We
must put away our tears, take off our mourning . . . and face the future," says Mommy.
"Brave Mommy!" says Daddy. Both are plainly
relieved to be rid of the old nuisance.

Albee uses absurdist stage devices to
symbolize a system gone awry, a culture

devoid of humanistic tradition and order.
Just as Mommy and Daddy's statements of grief
are feigned, so is the "funeral" itself
staged and phony. The guilt that should
accompany such mistreatment of a human being
is erased if the final rites are performed in
style—if one hires a musician to play and if
the Angel of Death is the most attractive the
studio has available. Empty ritual
substitutes for genuine human response, and
Grandma's funeral becomes a bad, unrehearsed
play. Mommy shouts into the wings to the
Musician: "You! Out there! You can come in
now." The Young Man interrupts Grandma to
say, "Uh . . . ma'am; I . . . I have a line
here." As a further affront to the illusion of
reality characteristic of drama born of more
stable cultures, Mommy, in response to an
offstage rumble, says, "It was an off-stage
rumble . . . and you know what that means."

This absurdist quality running throughout

the play suggests that in a world devoid of
ethical values, one "reality" is as good as
another. In a culture where human response is
governed by phony ritual and people care
absolutely nothing for one another, there is
no positive norm of reality for the artist to
exhibit. Such a world is as clumsily
mechanized and "unreal" as the robots who
inhabit it. When materialism has utterly
destroyed humanistic traditions, all human
activity is but bad playacting. Role-playing
replaces being, to the point where there are
no longer real people behind the masks and the
only reality is absurdity.

Albee's methods in The Sandbox may be
absurd, but his criticism of contemporary
American culture is frighteningly realistic.
America, daily sinking farther into the
slough of decadent materialism, is well
served by artists such as Albee who force us
to view our distorted images in the cracked

mirror of our sham values. One can only hope
that such vision hasn't come too late.

AIDS TO LITERARY ANALYSIS

Types of Papers

1. If a topic is assigned, it usually will be on a characteristic of literature which has been discussed previously in class. After introducing you to the function of imagery in a Browning poem, for instance, the instructor may ask you to write an analysis of the imagery in a poem by Tennyson. If a specific topic is assigned, be careful to focus your analysis on the literary quality which has been selected for you and not to write a general interpretation.

2. If the assignment is simply to write an analysis of a particular work of literature, you might limit your topic to a quality of the work which you consider especially significant or revealing—imagery, symbolism, a complex character, even a flaw in technique (see "Reflections Upon a Golden Eye").

3. Another type of paper is an overview of the total work. The overview, because it attempts to give an impression of the entire piece, is by necessity highly condensed. Selectivity is of the utmost importance, and the writer of an overview must concentrate on only the outstanding characters and events. Usually, the controlling idea of this type of analysis is the theme of the work and how it is developed through the protagonist. (See "Rock of Ages," "Where Have All the Flowers Gone?," "Deliverance from Evil," and "Boxed In.")

Writing Tips

1. Read shorter pieces, especially poems, several times before you attempt an analysis. If possible, allow some time to elapse between readings.

2. Just before writing, read the piece one last time and mark passages which you think you may be able to use in your analysis.

3. Then, using a rough outline, plan your paper and formulate an introductory paragraph. As in all expository essays, a literary analysis should open with some type of attention device followed by a clear, succinct statement of the controlling idea. The author and title of the work of literature you are writing about should be stated—but subordinated—somewhere in this opening paragraph. (See introductory paragraphs in the sample essays for examples.)

4. Some thought should be given to your title, either in the planning stage or immediately upon completing the essay. A catchy or revealing title is always an asset, either serving as an additional attention device or buttressing your thesis. A title such as "An Analysis of _____" is virtually worthless. Never use the title of the work you are analyzing as the title of your paper, and don't put your own title in quotation marks.

5. As you write, you may assume that your reader has read the selection you are analyzing. A retelling of the story is unnecessary and superfluous. Refer to details of the plot only to support or to illustrate your interpretation, always subordinating these details to your statements about their meaning.

6. Do not attempt to incorporate into your essay all the details you have marked. Use only the outstanding

and pertinent ones which can be worked into a natural, logical, and effective sequence of thought.

7. Slant each sentence in your analysis toward proving your thesis statement. The thread of thought expressed in this central idea must run through the entire paper. As an aid to maintaining focus on your controlling idea, or thesis, frequently repeat its key word or a synonym. As a check on yourself and a guide to your reader, make sure that each topic sentence develops some aspect of your thesis statement. Some writers even repeat a variation of their thesis statement at strategic points throughout the essay.

8. It is a convention of critical writing to refer to plot details in present-tense verbs. Therefore, you would write "Macbeth is an ambitious man" even though the play was written long ago and Macbeth dies at the end. When the play is read a hundred years from now, Macbeth will still be an ambitious man, and he will still be dying at the end. Historical and biographical facts mentioned in a critical essay are another matter. These are referred to in past-tense verbs, constituting a necessary—and correct—shift in tense. For example, you would write,

```
Nathaniel Hawthorne wrote [biographical
past tense] many stories about the Puritans,
who dominated [historical past tense] early
New England culture.  "Young Goodman Brown"
is [literary present tense] such a story.
```

9. In an analysis of a single work of literature, usually it is not necessary to footnote quotations and paraphrases or to give their page numbers within your paper. You must, however, introduce and smoothly incorporate quotations and paraphrases into your paper.

10. Because quotations must be kept proportionate to the length of the paper, there should be no long quotations in a short paper. Reduce a quoted passage to those details most pertinent to your point by using an ellipsis (. . .) to omit irrelevant material or by paraphrasing (stating the passage in your own words).

11. Except for indented quotations, place quotation marks around all directly quoted passages. Do not use quotation marks in an indented quotation unless the passage already includes quotation marks.

12. Indent poetry quotations of four lines or more and prose quotations of five lines or more. Quotations of this length should be kept at a minimum in short papers. Use the diagonal (/) to separate consecutive lines of poetry in nonindented quotations. Place the correct punctuation at the end of a quotation, but do not change any wording, capitalization, or punctuation within the quotation. Example: The conflict of "Stopping by Woods on a Snowy Evening" is expressed in the lines "The woods are lovely, dark and deep, / But I have promises to keep."

The
Handbook

1. ABBREVIATIONS

1. The general rule is to avoid abbreviations.

   a. In writing papers or business letters, do not abbreviate the days of the week, names of the months, states or countries, or such words as "Street" or "Avenue" in addresses.

   b. Do not use such common abbreviations as the following: Xmas, in., ft., doz., oz., lb., &, %, ¢, etc. (Also avoid the word "etcetera.")

2. The following abbreviations are acceptable:

   a. Abbreviate titles immediately preceding or immediately following a *full* name, such as these:

      Dr. G. T. Malloy
      Rev. J. B. Sternhaus
      Prof. George Wardlaw
      G. T. Malloy. M.D.
      J. B. Sternhaus, D.D.
      George Wardlaw, Ph.D.

      Note: When first names are omitted, do not abbreviate titles: Reverend Sternhaus.

   b. Abbreviate government agencies or organizations commonly known by their initials, such as FCC, HEW, CIA, NATO, CBS, ROTC, DAR, AFL-CIO.

   c. Abbreviate unusually long place-names, such as USSR and Washington, D.C.

   d. Abbreviate a.m. or p.m. following a figure: 8:30 a.m., 7:00 p.m.

   e. Abbreviate chemical formulas, such as H_2O, DDT, NaCl.

f. Abbreviate Mr., Mrs., and Ms.

2. ACTIVE VOICE/PASSIVE VOICE

Use the active voice to express most ideas.

In active-voice sentences, the subject does the acting:

Most of the students passed the test.

In passive-voice sentences, the subject is acted upon:

The test was passed by most of the students.

Careful writers avoid the passive voice because it is weaker and less emphatic than the active voice. There are, however, some valid uses of the passive voice:

1. Use the passive voice when you wish to emphasize the receiver of the action and not the "actor":

Joe was not admitted to law school.

2. You may use the passive voice when the "actor" is unimportant or obvious:

Carter was elected president in 1976.

3. You may use the passive voice when the "actor" is unknown:

My house was burglarized last night.

3. APOSTROPHES

1. For possessive case of nouns

a. Use an apostrophe before *s* to indicate possessive case of singular nouns and of plural nouns not ending in *s*:

Fred's, the dog's, a car's, a girl's, one parent's, oxen's, children's, men's, women's

Note: Possessive case of singular nouns already ending in s may be indicated by 's or by an apostrophe only: seamstress' or seamstress's, Keats's, Hopkins'. In quotations and article and book titles, you must preserve the original spelling of such words.

b. Use an apostrophe only to indicate possessive case of plural nouns already ending in s:

both cars', two girls', both parents', three churches', the Joneses'

c. Use an apostrophe before s for "idiomatic possessives" such as these:

a stone's throw, a week's time, a day's work

2. For possessive case of pronouns

a. Use an apostrophe with s to indicate the possessive case of indefinite pronouns such as "everybody's," "one's," "nobody's," "another's."

b. *Do not* use an apostrophe with possessive pronouns, such as "its," "his," "hers," "yours," "ours," or "theirs."

3. For omissions

a. Use an apostrophe to indicate the omission of a letter or letters in contractions:

I'm, isn't, can't, won't, we'll, you've, you're, it's ("It's" is the contraction of "it is"; the possessive pronoun "its" has no apostrophe.)

Note: Despite a lingering academic prejudice against contractions, they are now widely used in all types of writing.

b. Use an apostrophe to indicate the omission of letters in dialogue:

"I 'justed yo' brakes right the first time, and here you be grumblin' 'bout it,'' the old man sputtered.

4. For the plural of numbers and letters:

three 2 × 4's, two *B*'s and two *C*'s, *p*'s and *q*'s

Note: There is a trend toward omitting apostrophes from plural numbers: 1920s.

4. AWKWARDNESS

Avoid awkward wording and clumsy sentence structure.

An awkward sentence is one which is written in very poor style. Because awkwardness takes many different forms, there are no simple rules for solving this problem. Eliminating clumsy expressions depends primarily upon your developing an "ear" for the language—becoming aware of sound as well as sense. Proofreading your writing for sound, aloud when possible, can help you detect awkwardness. Awkward sentences *sound* bad, and they are almost always unclear.

Awkward:

A literal reading of the story may be made for entertainment.

Improved:

> The story may be read on the literal level for entertainment.

Awkward:

> To visualize a great athlete fascinates him as he pictures himself as one.

Improved:

> He is fascinated by his vision of himself as a great athlete.

Awkward:

> Much evidence of pollution appears in the campus newspaper, like the pictures on page one of the April 3 edition, where there are three.

Improved:

> Campus pollution is much in evidence. There are three pictures of polluted areas on the front page of the April 3 school newspaper.

Awkward:

> Kindness is attempted during Jim's visit with the Wingfields by both parties.

Improved:

> During the visit, Jim and the Wingfields try to be kind.

Unnatural expression creates awkward sentences. Avoid awkwardness by being yourself. Write as naturally as you can in your own "voice." Never write anything you wouldn't say, and try to be concise. Awkwardness and wordiness (see p. 378) often go hand in hand.

5. BRACKETS

Use brackets to enclose material you have inserted within a quotation.

Although such material may be a comment you wish to add, it is usually clarifying information or the editorial *sic*, which indicates an error, usually in spelling or grammar, in the quotation:

> Tennyson once said, "It ["Ulysses"] was more written with the feeling of his [Arthur Henry Hallam's] loss upon me than many poems in *In Memoriam*."

> According to the article, "Noblesse oblige" [responsible behavior associated with privileged rank] is not Billy Carter's strong point.

> The evaluation stated, "This teacher grades too strick [*sic*]."

Because brackets are somewhat awkward, they should be used only when absolutely necessary. The need for brackets usually can be eliminated by paraphrasing the quotation in your own words. If your typewriter does not have bracket keys, you must ink in the brackets. Parentheses *may not* substitute for brackets.

6. CAPITALS AND LOWERCASE

1. Capitalize the first word of a sentence, the personal pronoun "I," proper names (Amy, Spot, Mr. Cornett, the Chinese), place-names of all types (Russia, New York, The Stork Club), holidays (Thanksgiving, St. Patrick's Day), dates (Friday, August 30), and periods of time (Medieval Period, Age of Romanticism, Stone Age, Jazz Age).

2. Also observe the following conventions of capitalization and lowercase:

    a. Capitalize subjects of study only when they are a language or part of a formal course title:

    > I'm taking French and biology.
    >
    > I'm taking Biology 101.

    b. Capitalize names of academic classes only when they are part of a title:

    > I'm just a freshman now, but I hope to be elected to the Sophomore Council next year.

    c. Capitalize seasons only when they are part of a title:

    > It looks like spring has finally arrived.
    >
    > I plan to graduate Spring Semester, 1988.

    d. Capitalize words indicating relationship or occupation only when they are used as titles:

    > Tell me, Mom, what was your mom like?
    >
    > Did you say that Coach Williams is the new soccer coach?

    e. Capitalize "north," "south," "east," and "west" when they are used as proper names for geographical areas and do not capitalize them when they indicate a direction:

    > The American South is rich in history and legend.
    >
    > The wind is blowing from the south.

    f. Capitalize names of racial, religious, and political groups:

Martin Luther King, a Negro Baptist minister, was a leading Democrat. Oddly, his fight for freedom resulted in the accusation that he was a Communist.

However, do not capitalize ideological words when they do not refer to a formal group:

There has been a long struggle between communism and democracy.

g. Capitalize the first, the last, and all important words in all types of titles:

Vice-President of Internal Affairs

War of the Roses

The Old Man and the Sea

"The Charge of the Light Brigade"

National Association for the Advancement of Colored People

h. Capitalize the first word of dialogue, whether or not it is a complete sentence:

George said, "You can't do this to me!"

"Not if I can help it!" Sally retorted.

i. Capitalize the first word of a fully quoted sentence:

According to Thomas Hardy, "If you look beneath the surface of any farce, you see a tragedy."

j. Do not begin a partial quotation incorporated into a sentence with a capital unless the quotation already begins with a capital:

Thomas Hardy said that "beneath the surface of any farce you see a tragedy."

But:

> Browning's duke condemns his wife for being "Too easily impressed." [capitalized in the poem].

7. CHOPPINESS

Avoid choppy sentences.

A short sentence can be effective, especially if a series of longer ones lead up to it, as in this example:

> Toe to fang with a coiled rattler for the first time in my life, all my nightmares came true. I'd always been insanely afraid of snakes, even harmless ones, and had tried to allay my fears by learning all I could about them. The woodlore wisdom of "don't panic, don't make sudden movements, remain perfectly still" flashed through my mind, but my body paid it no heed. It trembled shamelessly.

Several short sentences in a row, however, usually indicate that the writer has not taken the time to show the relationship of ideas by means of subordination (see p. 358) and coordination (see p. 291). A choppy effect results, as in these examples:

Choppy:

> The Maine coast is unique. I spent my summer vacation there. It isn't like the rest of the Atlantic coastline. It has large rocks. They look wild and primitive. The water is very cold. It's cold even in midsummer. One day it was 56°. It was posted on a sign. The sun was hot. There were many sunbathers. There were only a few swimmers. The water was too chilly.

Improved:

>The Maine coast, where I spent my summer vacation, is unique. Unlike the rest of the Atlantic shore, Maine's coastline is studded with giant boulders, giving it a wild and primitive appearance. Another difference is the coldness of the water, even in midsummer. Water temperature, posted regularly at the beach I visited, dropped to 56° one day. The warm sun drew a myriad of sunbathers, but only the hardy few braved the chilling waters.

Choppy:

>"Birches" was written by Robert Frost. It is about carefree youth. It is also about troubled adulthood. "Birches" contrasts the two.

Improved:

>"Birches," by Robert Frost, contrasts carefree youth with troubled adulthood.

In this second example, note that combining ideas eliminates wordiness as well as choppiness.

8. CLICHÉS

To make your writing as fresh and as imaginative as possible, avoid cliché expressions—such as "agonizing reappraisal," "mount an offensive," "winter wonderland," "tropical paradise," "cold as ice," "hard as a rock," "white as a sheet," and "glitters like gold." Also avoid trite ideas like these:

Money doesn't grow on trees.

Money can't buy happiness.

My dream became a reality.

You can't judge a book by its cover.

Every cloud has a silver lining.

Winners never quit.

I just want to make others happy.

If you try your best, you can do anything in the world.

If you have heard an expression—especially a figurative comparison—over and over again, don't use it.

9. COLONS

1. Use a colon after a statement introducing a list:

    Before cutting firewood, you will need these items: a chain saw, gasoline, oil, an axe, a wedge, goggles, and earplugs.

2. Use a colon after a statement introducing a quotation:

    a. Ben Franklin coined a proverb which has haunted many a schoolboy: "Early to bed and early to rise makes a man healthy, wealthy, and wise."

    b. G.K. Chesterton has high praise for Dickens' imagination:

    This is the first and last dignity of Dickens; that he was a creator. . . . We may disapprove of Mr. Guppy, but we recognize him as a creation flung down like a miracle out of an upper sphere; we can pull him to pieces, but we could not have put him together.

    Strictly speaking, a colon is used only after introductory *statements*—that is, main (independent) clauses.

If the introductory material is a dependent clause or phrase, it is followed by a comma and not a colon, even if the quotation introduced is long enough to be indented:

> Benjamin Franklin said, "Early to bed and early to rise makes a man healthy, wealthy, and wise."

In praise of Dickens' imagination, G.K. Chesterton says,

> This is the first and last dignity of Dickens; that he was a creator. . . . We may disapprove of Mr. Guppy, but we recognize him as a creation flung down like a miracle out of an upper sphere; we can pull him to pieces, but we could not have put him together.

Note: A popular modern exception to this rule is the use of colons after elliptical introductions:

> Example: (Shortening of "Here is an example.")
> His best-known work: (Shortening of "This is his best-known work.")

3. Use a colon after a statement which clearly introduces the following word, phrase, or clause:

> Then I discovered the source of my irritation: chiggers.
>
> There was only one thing left to do: run for my life.
>
> Mulling over the alternatives, I reached a decision: discretion is the better part of valor.

Note: The less formal dash (—) is now widely used as an alternative to the colon in this type of sentence.

4. Use a colon after the greeting in a business letter:

Dear Dean Fogerty:
Dear Sirs:
Editor:
Boxholder:

10. COMMAS

1. a. Use a comma before a coordinating conjunction ("and," "but," "or," "for," "nor," "so," and "yet") connecting two main clauses. (For a definition of a main clause, see p. 288.)

> He waved to his sister, and his mother waved back.
> You can study and learn, or you can cheat and remain ignorant.

Note: If the two main clauses are very short and there is no chance of misreading, the comma may be omitted:

> I competed and I lost.
> Joan came but Bill didn't.

b. If the coordinating conjunction does not join *two* main clauses, a comma is not used:

> He waved to his sister and his mother.
> You can study or cheat.

2. Use a comma to separate elements in a series:

> Math, chemistry, and English are difficult subjects.
> We hiked, swam, and loafed.
> The young, inexperienced, but spirited team won its first game.

A good defensive lineman is agile, mobile, and hostile.

3. Use a comma to set off an introductory word, phrase, or clause:

Surprisingly, Jimmy did not press his advantage.

Seeing the straight flush, I tossed in my cards.

Because I had worked hard all day, I left the party early.

4. Use a comma to set off transitional words and phrases:

I can't stand this job any longer. Therefore, I'm resigning as of this moment.

I had a long session with my psychiatrist yesterday. As a result, I'm quitting school.

When transitional words and phrases appear within sentences, they are set off by a pair of commas:

Mary, however, didn't see it that way.

Vandalism, on the other hand, is a senseless crime.

As a quick test for correct use of commas in pairs, see if the single words, phrases, or dependent clauses enclosed by commas could be omitted without damage to grammar or basic meaning, as they could be in these examples:

My youngest brother, Dan, is staying with me.

Mr. Morris, by working every spare minute, built his own home.

Studying, although it can be boring, usually pays off.

5. Use a pair of commas to set off mild sentence interrupters:

> Jimmy, surprisingly enough, did not press his advantage.
>
> Johnnie, according to the news media, can't read.
>
> She said it, granted, but did she mean it?
>
> That, to my way of thinking, is an outlandish statement.

6. Commas with appositives

   a. Use a comma to set off a nonrestrictive appositive (a noun or noun phrase which identifies or describes the noun it follows, but which is not strictly necessary to the meaning of the sentence):

   > Virginia gave us our first president, *Washington.*
   >
   > One of the most tragic figures in sports is Roy Campanella, *the great Dodger catcher.*

   If a nonrestrictive appositive occurs *within* the sentence, it is set off by a pair of commas:

   > Our first president, *Washington,* was from Virginia.
   >
   > Roy Campanella, *the great Dodger catcher,* had his career cut short by an automobile accident.

   In all these sentences, the appositives are nonrestrictive because they could be omitted without loss of basic meaning.

   b. *Do not* use commas with a restrictive appositive (a noun or noun phrase which identifies or describes the noun it follows and is necessary to the meaning of the sentence):

The great baseball player Roy Campanella was disabled in an automobile accident. (The appositive, "Roy Campanella," is needed to identify which baseball player is referred to.)

Robert Frost's poem "Birches" is about the loss of innocence. (The appositive, "Birches," is needed to identify which poem by Frost is being discussed.)

7. Commas with relative clauses

a. Use a comma to set off a nonrestrictive relative (adjective) clause (a clause which identifies or describes the noun it follows, but which is not strictly necessary to the meaning of the sentence):

I owe a lot to my father, *who taught me the value of work.*

I enjoyed Tolkien's last novel, *which I just read.*

If a nonrestrictive clause appears within a sentence, it is set off by a pair of commas:

My father, *who taught me the value of work,* is a brickmason.

Tolkien's last novel, *which I just read,* is a fascinating book.

b. *Do not* use commas with a restrictive relative clause (a clause which modifies the noun it follows and is necessary to the meaning of the sentence):

The man *who taught me the value of work* is my father.

Freshman English is a course *that almost everyone needs.*

Both clauses are restrictive because the basic meaning of each sentence would be lost if they were omitted.

8. Use a comma to separate direct quotations from "tag lines" identifying the speaker or writer:

"I don't understand," Gerald replied.

Pope wrote, "A little learning is a dangerous thing."

"Tag lines" within quotations are set off by a pair of commas:

"Nothing," Harriet said, "will make me change my mind."

"A little learning," wrote Mr. Pope, "is a dangerous thing."

9. Use a comma to set off mild interjections:

Well, maybe he's right.

Yes, you heard correctly.

10. Use commas to set off nouns of direct address:

Scott, please shut the door and your mouth.

Tell me, Joe, why did you do it?

11. Use commas to separate the day, month, and year in dates:

Brian was born on Tuesday, March 3, 1970.

March 28, 1942, is an important date to me.

12. Use a comma to separate city from state and city from country in place-names:

Chapel Hill, North Carolina, is the site of a state university.

Bangkok, Thailand, is a beautiful place.

13. Use a comma to set off a title following a name:

    Steadman Smith, M.D., heads the Heart Fund.

    N.F. Shrewsbury, Professor of English, is my advisor.

14. Use a comma after the greeting in a personal letter:

    Hi Susie,

    Dear Mom,

15. Use a comma to separate sentence parts:

    I was happy to see everyone, in particular John and Sally.

    One committee member is always a student, usually a senior.

    I was tired, but nonetheless happy.

    Paul seemed excited, as well as a bit angry.

    A bigot is a bigot, even if he has money and prestige.

There are so many varieties of sentences which require comma separation of sentence parts that there are no specific comma rules governing them. For correct punctuation of such sentences, an instinctive sense of where the sentence "breaks" is required. The "voice pause" test usually is a reliable aid.

Commas generally correspond to slight pauses, just as periods correspond to full stops. Read over your composition, and listen. At places where your voice naturally pauses, you probably need a comma. If you have a comma where there is no pause in your reading voice, you probably should remove it.

11. COMMA SPLICES

Do not join sentences with a comma.

A comma splice occurs when a comma is placed at the end of a sentence instead of the correct "stop" or "end" punctuation (usually a period, but also a question mark, an exclamation point, or, in some special types of sentences, a semicolon or a colon). Using a comma instead of one of these marks of punctuation causes two sentences to be "spliced" together.

To avoid comma splices (as well as fragments), you must be able to distinguish between main (independent) clauses and subordinate (dependent) clauses. A main clause is a structure that either is a sentence or *could be* a sentence if it were written alone.

The structure "I was sick, but I went to class anyhow" contains two main clauses. Both "I was sick" and "I went to class anyhow" could stand alone as sentences. Each has a subject and a predicate, and neither has a subordinating element which makes it dependent upon a larger structure in order to be grammatical. The two main clauses have been joined by the coordinating conjunction "but," preceded by a comma. However, they could have been written separately: "I was sick. I went to class anyhow."

The structure "Although I was sick" entirely changes the grammar of the sentence. "Although I was sick," in spite of the fact that it has a subject and a predicate, is a dependent clause because of the subordinating word "although." "Although I was sick" could not stand alone as a sentence. It must be attached to a main clause in order to be a grammatical part of a sentence: "Although I was sick, I went to class anyhow." Note the comma separating the subordinate from the main clause.

Once you have learned to iden
proofreading aid will help you elim

Possible Punctuat

Main clause	.	Main clause
	;	
	?	
	!	
	:	
	, and	
	, but	
	, or	
	, for	
	, nor	
	, so	
	, yet	

1. Comma splices often are caused by confusing transitional adverbs such as "however," therefore," "nevertheless," and "thus" with the coordinating conjunctions "and," "but," "or," "for," "nor," "so," and "yet." Coordinating conjunctions, as the name implies, *can* join two main clauses; transitional adverbs cannot.

This sentence is correct:

A college degree can be useful, but some people simply aren't capable of earning one.

This sentence has a comma splice:

A college degree can be useful, however some people simply aren't capable of earning one.

Corrected:

A college degree can be useful. However, some people simply aren't capable of earning one.

r:

A college degree can be useful; however, some people simply aren't capable of earning one.

To avoid this type of comma splice, remember that only the coordinating conjunctions "and," "but," "or," "for," "nor," "so," and "yet" can be used to join two main clauses.

Another type of comma splice results from the use of a comma to separate two main clauses which are closely related in thought:

Some people find ways to better themselves, others just complain.   ;

Though these two statements are closely related, a comma alone cannot be used to separate them. If you wish to stress the unity of these two thoughts, you may join them by means of a comma *and* a coordinating conjunction:

Some people find ways to better themselves, but others just complain.

Another way to stress the unity of two separate statements is to place a semicolon between them:

Some people find ways to better themselves; others just complain.

When a semicolon is used between two main clauses, the coordinating conjunction is usually omitted.

A period may always be used to separate two declarative main clauses:

Some people find ways to better themselves. Others just complain.

3. In literary analysis papers, comma splices sometimes result from incorrect punctuation after a statement introducing a quotation:

Hulga then shows that she shares some of her mother's naiveté, "Aren't you just good country people?" she asks.

The correct punctuation following a *statement* introducing a quotation is a colon, which eliminates the comma splice:

Hulga then shows that she shares some of her mother's naiveté: "Aren't you just good country people?" she asks.

If, however, the introduction of the quotation is *not* a statement, a comma is correct:

Then Hulga asks, "Aren't you just good county people?"

12. COORDINATION

Make sentence parts which are equal in thought coordinate, or parallel, in grammatical form.

1. Error in coordination (failure to balance equal ideas):

Harold being in a grumpy mood and Joe was tired, we decided to stay home.

Revision (with parallel elements in italics):

Because *Harold was grumpy* and *Joe was tired,* we decided to stay home.

Error in coordination:

My favorite sports are tennis and football, billiards being a favorite, too.

Revision:

My favorite sports are *tennis, football,* and *billiards.* (Elements in a series must be parallel in form.)

Error in coordination:

Most people see themselves as they would like to be instead of what they are.

Revision:

Most people see themselves *as they would like to be* instead of *as they are.*

Error in coordination (needless shift from active to passive voice):

After the victory, the team was tired, but happiness was felt, too.

Revision:

After the victory, the team was *tired* but *happy.*

Be especially alert to the need for parallelism—that is, balanced forms—in sentences with coordinating conjunctions (and, but, or, for, nor, so, yet).

2. Faulty coordination (balancing unequal ideas):

Bill Hoxey is an old classmate of mine, and he has a novel on the bestseller list.

The two ideas of this sentence are given equal emphasis by parallel sentence structure. A more logical statement would deemphasize the fact that Bill is an old classmate and emphasize his success as an author:

Bill Hoxey, an old classmate of mine, has a novel on the bestseller list.

Do not give equal emphasis to unequal ideas. State important ideas in main clauses; make lesser ideas subordinate in structure. (See Subordination, p. 358.)

13. DANGLING MODIFIERS

Place modifying words and phrases as close as possible to the words they modify and make sure that the words modified are stated in the sentence.

1. Most dangling modifiers are phrases at the beginning of sentences.

Wrong:

Driving to school this morning, my car was involved in an accident. (This sentence has the car doing the driving.)

Revision:

Driving to school this morning, I was involved in an accident.

Wrong:

Warned about a pop test, my studying became frantic. ("Studying" is warned.)

Revision:

Warned about a pop test, I studied frantically.

Wrong:

If elected governor, the senior citizens of this state will be treated better. (Senior citizens are running for governor.)

Revision:

If elected governor, I will see to it that the senior citizens of this state are treated better.

2. A dangling modifier may be a single word.

Wrong:

Angered, an argument ensued between us. ("Angered" incorrectly modifies "argument.")

Revision:

Angered, we got into an argument.

Wrong:

Reluctantly, the date was called off. ("Reluctantly" improperly modifies "date.")

Revision:

Reluctantly, we called off the date.

Remembering this rule will help you eliminate dangling modifiers: **When a sentence begins with a modifying word or phrase, the noun or pronoun following the modifier must be the thing modified.**

14. DASHES

1. Use a dash to set off an explanation or comment which abruptly interrupts the flow of a sentence:

> The new football coach is Jimmy Brown—not the Jimmy Brown who was a star in the pros.
>
> I am—make no mistake about it—not a crook.

Note that dashes are used in pairs to set off interruptions *within* sentences.

2. Use a dash to indicate sudden shift in thought or an ironic turn:

> When the bell rang, Professor Goodheart said, "You must turn in your papers—no, take them home and finish them."
>
> I have great faith in advertising firms—faith that they'll do anything to sell their products.

3. Use a dash to show interrupted dialogue:

> "I'll give you your money just as soon as—"
>
> "It's too late now!" Jaggers broke in.

4. Except in formal writing such as research, a dash may be used in place of a colon after an introductory remark:

> I then returned to my favorite pastime—sleeping.
>
> I had one last thing to do—proofread my paper.

In order to distinguish dashes from hyphens, in typing use the double hyphen (--) and in handwriting make dashes twice as long as hyphens (—).

15. DEVELOPMENT

Supply supporting and clarifying information.

1. Unsupported generalizations

Always support generalizations by analyzing evidence and presenting concrete examples. Generalizations without supporting details create the impression that you have not thought out your ideas. An unsupported generalization in writing is the equivalent of a lawyer's saying "My client is innocent" or a politician's saying "I am the best man for the job." Such statements remain empty opinions until they are backed by specific data. The following paragraphs lack concrete supporting details:

English is a waste of time. There is simply no need for it. I'm a business major, and I see no point in wasting valuable time in English courses.

Learning to write is very important. Communication skills will help a person get ahead in the world. Writing is one of the most important things that can be learned in college.

No homemaker should be without a Sooper-Dooper Blender. I know you'll want to invest in one. You'll be proud to own this little dandy. A Sooper-Dooper on your shelf means time on your hands!

2. Unclarified statement

Some statements, especially those making bold or "profound" assertions, may be insufficiently developed because their meaning is not completely clear. Such statements often sound more thoughtful than they are. In this case, you must explain and clarify your meaning by commenting further and by supplying supporting details, such as examples and illustrations.

Your ability to develop and clarify such statements will determine whether they are real insights. A sentence such as "Senator Krupp resembles an absurdist escapee from a Kurt Vonnegut novel" sounds impressive, but exactly what is meant by "absurdist"? How do Vonnegut's characters illustrate the definition? In what specific ways does Senator Krupp resemble them? Good writers supply the answers to such questions.

Don't expect your reader to fill in gaps for you. You must write into your papers all the details your audience will need to follow your line of thought. It is always better to give too much information than too little. The best writers, of course, give just enough.

Insufficient knowledge of your subject is not an excuse for lack of development. You should not attempt to write on subjects about which you know little. Additional information may be gathered by observation, reading, or interviewing authorities, but don't hesitate to abandon a subject if you lack the information to develop it.

3. Example of a well supported and clearly developed paragraph:

> For many people, the college years are the most carefree they'll ever experience. Consider these advantages. Parents pay most of the typical student's bills. In contrast to the past, many college students now have cars. Freed from the burden of earning a living and blessed with greater mobility, most modern college students enjoy a social life envied by their less fortunate high school classmates chained to low-paying jobs. Sporting events, dances, concerts,

and cultural programs are available right on campus, easily accessible even to those without transportation. As far as dating goes, never again will a person mingle with so many eligible members of the opposite sex. Many colleges now permit drinking and closed-door "visitation" on campus, privileges some students may not have been allowed at home. Many different life-styles and living arrangements are also available to the modern student, freedoms which may be curtailed after graduation. The buttoned-down junior executive or the prim and proper schoolteacher may look back on the less restrictive days of college with nostalgia. When a person starts a family and responsibilities mount, the difference between the adult world and college becomes even more apparent. In short, the typical modern college student enjoys most of the freedoms of adulthood and is burdened with almost none of its duties.

16. DIAGONALS

1. Use a diagonal to show division between two or three lines of quoted poetry:

> Wordsworth, an early opponent of materialism, says, "Getting and spending, we lay waste our powers; / Little we see in Nature that is ours."

2. Use a diagonal to show divisions even if the lines aren't fully quoted:

> Wordsworth writes that "we lay waste our powers; / Little we see in Nature that is ours."

In quoting poetry (or prose), the punctuation and capitalization of the original must be preserved. In quoting consecutive lines of poetry, any punctuation within and between the lines must be preserved. At the end of a quotation, however, use the punctuation which makes *your own* writing correct. For instance, preserving a comma which appears at the end of a quoted passage would result in a comma splice if you then began a new sentence in your paper. The correct punctuation at the end of a quotation almost always is a period.

Indent, or block, poetry quotations of four lines or more. *Diagonals are not used in blocked poetry quotations.*

17. DICTION

Use words which state your meaning exactly, which are appropriate to your tone and subject, and which are not repetitious in sound.

The general rule for diction is to choose the simplest and clearest words possible. Don't try to impress your readers with a big word when a shorter one gets the job done. On the other hand, if a longer word carries the exact shade of meaning you want, then use it. For instance, "happy" is a shorter, simpler word than "jubilant," but a writer may want the stronger connotation of happiness achieved by the longer word in a sentence such as "Sue was jubilant after winning the new Corvette."

In addition to conveying the precise shade of meaning you want, your language should also be appropriate to your subject and to the audience you hope to reach. (See Tone and Audience, p. 17.) Good diction is simple, accurate, and appropriate language. Yet another consideration is sound. Most papers aren't read aloud, but sounds are "heard" in the mind of your reader. Vary wording to avoid unpleasant repetition of sound.

The better your vocabulary, the greater your chances of selecting the right word. As your vocabulary builds, your writing should become more precise. But don't force it. You must use only those words whose meaning you are sure of—both the denotation, or literal meaning, and the connotation, or emotional associations a word can carry. Consider the difference between merely being contented and being exhilarated, or between feeling melancholy and feeling depressed. Most of us like to be called youthful, but we resent being called immature. Such shades of meaning make a crucial difference.

A thesaurus (dictionary of synonyms) may help you locate just the word you want, but you must use a thesaurus carefully or you will merely substitute one bad word choice for another. Never select a word from a thesaurus unless you are sure of its exact meaning and never, but never, use a thesaurus to "fancy up" your writing vocabulary. One of the surest ways to lose your readers is to write in a pretentious, inflated style.

1. Use exact words.

    a. Avoid inaccurate expressions. In the following examples, the inexact word choice is italicized and a more accurate word is given in brackets:

    There was nothing to do, so we drove to a movie in a *surrounding* [nearby] town.

    Death is almost always a sad *situation* [experience].

    High school and college differ in several *aspects* [respects].

    Using the wrong fork at a formal dinner can be *shameful* [embarrassing].

    I appreciated the gift even though it was *cheap* [inexpensive].

Kafka's hunger artist *obtains* [achieves] meaning through fasting.

b. Avoid inflated expressions. (See Wordiness on p. 378. Poor diction and wordiness often occur together.)

Inflated:

Miss Fitzhugh, my English teacher in high school, is a servant of humanity, a paragon of virtue, and a credit to the human race.

Improved:

Miss Fitzhugh, my English teacher in high school, is a wonderful person.

Inflated:

Pressure can stimulate responses that are not commensurate with a person's normal behavior.

Improved:

Under pressure, people sometimes do things they usually wouldn't do.

Inflated:

Graduation from high school was a fantastically glorious yet heartrending experience which I shall cherish down through the annals of time.

Improved:

I don't think I'll ever forget the joy or the sadness of my high school graduation.

Inflated:

Many first-graders are disadvantaged, underprepared, and emotionally inadequate to a learning situation.

Improved:

Many first-graders aren't ready for school.

Inflated:

In "The Horse-Dealer's Daughter," Mabel experiences an overwhelming uplift at the doctor's intimation of love, and an antisuicidal fortitude is engendered.

Improved:

In "The Horse-Dealer's Daughter," Mabel's realization that the doctor loves her gives her the strength to go on living.

2. Use appropriate words.

a. Avoid sexist references. Many readers are offended by general references such as "man" or "mankind" and by masculine pronouns and male occupational terms used to refer to both men and women. Such expressions result from habit and long practice, and while usually no offense is intended, these references are nonetheless discriminatory and likely to alienate a number of your readers.

Sexist nouns and pronouns almost always can be avoided without creating awkwardness or resorting to such self-conscious, unpleasant terms as "personkind" or "chairperson," as these examples illustrate:

Sexist:

If mankind is to survive, we must develop new forms of energy.

Nonsexist:

>If humanity is to survive, we must develop new forms of energy.

Sexist:

>Man is a strange animal.

Nonsexist:

>Humans are strange animals.

Sexist:

>Most congressmen were off campaigning for reelection.

Nonsexist:

>Most members of Congress were off campaigning for reelection.

Sexist:

>Outgoing chairman Janice Wellborn turned the gavel over to the newly elected chairman, Nate Hampton.

Nonsexist:

>Outgoing chairwoman Janice Wellborn turned the gavel over to the newly elected chairman, Nate Hampton.

Sexist:

>If the reader wants to review the main ideas of a theme, he can look back over the topic sentences.

Nonsexist:

>If readers want to review the main ideas of a

theme, they can look back over the topic sentences.

b. Avoid slang. The best reason to avoid slang is that it is "language peculiar to a particular group" (*Webster's New Collegiate Dictionary*), and you should aim your essays at as large an audience as possible. Slang can be lively, but popular slang expressions quickly become overused and outdated. The slang terms which are still fresh may puzzle many of your readers. Therefore, as a general rule, you should avoid the use of slang in serious expository writing. Use a slang term only when it is the very best way to communicate your meaning and when it does not disrupt the overall style of your paper.

(1) Tone-breakers. The slang terms in the following examples do not fit the style of the passages:

Slang:

Albert Schweitzer devoted most of his life to helping others. That *dude* was *something else.*

Improved:

Albert Schweitzer devoted most of his life to helping others. He was quite a man.

Slang:

Gloria Steinem has worked hard for the *libbers.* She's a *cool chick.*

Improved:

Gloria Steinem has worked hard for sexual equality. She's an impressive woman.

Slang:

> The church has produced some excellent music. "Amazing Grace," for instance, is a *dynamite* hymn.

Improved:

> The church has produced some excellent music. "Amazing Grace," for instance, is a fine old hymn.

Slang:

> T.S. Eliot's "The Waste Land" is considered a great poem, but I think it's a real *bummer.*

Improved:

> T.S. Eliot's "The Waste Land" is considered a great poem, but I detest it.

(2) Jargon. The various professions constantly invent special terms or catchwords for their activities. Such terms almost always replace clearer, more standard words and lack even the momentary appeal of popular slang. Unfortunately, these pretentious invaders often creep into general use, where they quickly become clichés. Jargon is a special type of professional slang. Don't use it.

Jargon:

> To make *ongoing* improvements, management needs the *input* of employees.

Improved:

> To make continuous improvements, management needs the ideas of employees.

Jargon:

> The committee needs more *feedback* in order to *finalize* its recommendations.

Improved:

> The committee needs more information in order to complete its recommendations.

Jargon:

> We must *prioritize* our objectives in order to *impact upon* the *active child*.

Improved:

> We've got to do something about unruly children.

Jargon:

> Spitspear is *some kind of* pitcher. He has tremendous *velocity*.

Improved:

> Spitspear is an outstanding pitcher. He throws hard.

Jargon:

> We're not *relating*. I'm not sure *where you're coming from*.

Improved:

> What do you mean?

(3) Vulgarities. The type of slang commonly referred to as "four-letter words" should be avoided in expository writing. A good writer doesn't have to

shock or offend in order to get a reaction. Writers can't be squeamish, but neither should they be needlessly and self-consciously offensive. Virtually the only time a vulgar expression is justified in expository writing is in the instance of dialogue to reveal character in a character sketch or narrative. Even in this special case, realism must be an overriding factor, and constant use of vulgar terms may create the impression that the writer is more interested in a juvenile attempt to shock than in realism.

3. Do not use repetitious words. Avoid unpleasant repetition of sound by following these principles:

    a. Avoid using the same word twice in a sentence. Also avoid using two words formed from the same root within one sentence.

    Unpleasant repetition:

        Many critics *describe* Hemingway as a *realistic* writer because of his *realistic descriptions* of such experiences as sports, war, and crime.

    Improved:

        Many critics consider Hemingway a realist because of his true-to-life accounts of such experiences as sports, war, and crime.

    b. Avoid using two words which sound alike in the same sentence, even if the words are different in meaning.

    Unpleasant repetition:

        Some educators *object* to stated course *objectives*,

but these goals *formally inform* students of learning aims.

Improved:

Some educators don't like stated course objectives, but these goals concretely inform students of learning aims.

Before writing down a sentence, turn it over in your mind and listen to its sound. A thesaurus can help you achieve variety in diction, but remember to use only those words whose exact meaning you are sure of.

18. ELLIPSES

1. Use ellipses to indicate an omission in a quoted passage in research writing. The ellipsis (three spaced periods) is a very useful mark of punctuation in research papers. It enables you to eliminate parts of quotations which are not pertinent to your specific topic. Such omissions often are necessary for coherence, and any paper with extensive quotations from which nothing has been omitted is almost certain to include irrelevant material.

Omissions within sentences are marked by three spaced periods plus any internal punctuation, such as commas, which may be required. Omissions at the ends of sentences are marked by the three spaced periods preceded by the mark of end punctuation for the sentence, usually a period. Omission of an entire sentence or of several sentences within a passage is indicated by four spaced periods.

Original passage (from *Poetry and the Age*):

Man without myth, without God, without anything but the universe which has produced him, is given an extraordinarily pure and touching grandeur in these lines—lines as beautiful, perhaps, as any in American poetry.

With omissions:

Randall Jarrell says that in "Sunday Morning," by Wallace Stevens, "Man . . . is given an extraordinarily pure and touching grandeur. . . ."

The first dot is a period indicating a complete statement. Note that there is no space preceding the period. If an ellipsis at the end of a nonindented quotation is followed by a reference in parentheses, the sentence punctuation is placed *after* the parentheses:

Randall Jarrell says that in "Sunday Morning," by Wallace Stevens, "Man . . . is given an extraordinarily pure and touching grandeur . . ." (p. 99).

In making omissions you must be careful not to distort the original meaning of a quoted passage, as has been done in this example:

Randall Jarrell says that "God . . . has produced . . . an extraordinarily pure and touching grandeur. . . ."

You must also take care that omissions do not result in ungrammatical or nonsense sentences, as in this example:

Randall Jarrell says that "without myth . . . has produced . . . an extraordinarily pure and touching grandeur. . . ."

2. Use ellipses to indicate an omission in quoting a passage from literature.

   Original passage (from "The Love Song of J. Alfred Prufrock"):

   Though I have seen my head (grown slightly bald) brought in upon a platter.

   Incorporated into paper with omissions:

   Prufrock, alluding to John the Baptist, says, "I have seen my head . . . brought in upon a platter."

   Note that in both literary and research writing, omissions at the beginning of a passage, especially if they are insignificant, usually are not marked by ellipses. Ellipses are omitted altogether in quoting single words and phrases because they would be redundant and awkward:

   Dylan Thomas' "The Force That Through the Green Fuse Drives the Flower" is filled with images of death, such as "crooked rose," "wintry fever," "quicksand," "shroud," "clay," "hangman's lime," "fallen blood," and "crooked worm."

3. Use ellipses to show halting or broken speech in dialogue:

   "I don't know what came over me," Ted whimpered. "I drank too much. Then . . . then Kaye insulted me and . . . How can I face all those people who . . ."

4. Use ellipses to indicate an intentionally incomplete thought or ending:

   There *is* something in a Sunday . . .

   Surely we'll clean up the air before it kills us . . .

19. EXCLAMATION POINTS

1. Use an exclamation point after declarative expressions of strong feeling:

   It's time we stood up for our rights!

   Please say you love me!

   Get out of here and leave me alone!

   "Ouch!" he exclaimed.

   Don't let me hear you use the word "feedback"!

2. Use an exclamation point after expressions of strong feeling, even when they are worded as questions:

   Will you please come in out of the rain!

   How can you say that!

   Exclamations, like underlining for emphasis, lose their effect if overused. Use them sparingly.

20. FIGURES

1. a. Use figures for dates: August 30, 1973 (but the *third* of July).
   b. Use figures for times with a.m. or p.m.: 6:00 a.m. (but six o'clock).
   c. Use figures for addresses: 232 East Street (but 621 Second Avenue).
   d. Use figures for numbers which would require several words to write out, such as $8,260, 50.6 percent, 130 mph, 5'9", 220 pounds, 5,280 feet, 1¼ inches, 9,223 students.

2. a. Do not use figures for a number which can be expressed in one or two words, such as ten thousand dollars, fifty percent, ninety mph, six feet tall, a

hundred pounds, a thousand yards, one-fourth cup, twenty-five students.

b. Do not use figures at the beginning of a sentence.

Incorrect:

4,236 students are enrolled in summer school.

Since it is awkward to express large numbers in words, such sentences should be rewritten to place the number somewhere other than first:

There are 4,236 students enrolled in summer school.

Summer school enrollment is 4,236 students.

However, a sentence may begin with a short number if it is written out:

Ninety-six students failed English 101 last year.

21. FRAGMENTS

Use complete sentences.

A sentence fragment is a nonsentence (a fragment of a sentence) which is written as if it were a sentence. (That is, it begins with a capital letter and ends with "stop" punctuation, usually a period.)

A sentence must contain at least one main (independent) clause. (See discussion of main clauses on p. 288.) A sentence fragment is easy to detect in isolation. In the context of other related ideas, however, fragments may not be so obvious, so examine each sentence separately when proofreading.

There are two common causes of fragments:

1. Mistaking a word which looks like a verb for a predicate.

   > We decided not to go to the party. John *being* in a bad mood.

   "We decided not to go to the party" is a sentence, but "John being in a bad mood" is a fragment. It has a subject (John), but to function as a predicate, a verb form ending in "-ing" must have an auxiliary, or "helping," verb, as in "You are being silly." The fragment may be eliminated by incorporating it into the previous sentence:

   > John being in a bad mood, we decided not to go to the party.

   Or by changing the verbal "being" to a full verb:

   > John was in a foul mood, so we decided not to go to the party.

2. Mistaking a dependent clause for an independent (main) clause.

   > I didn't object very strenuously. Because, to tell the truth, I really didn't care.

   "Because, to tell the truth, I really didn't care" has a subject (I) and a predicate (didn't care), but the subordinating word "because" makes it a dependent clause and therefore a fragment when written alone. The fragment may be eliminated by joining it to the main clause:

   > I didn't object very strenuously because, to tell the truth, I really didn't care.

   Or by omitting the subordinating word:

I didn't object very strenuously. To tell the truth, I really didn't care.

Beware of clauses which begin with such subordinating words as "whereas," "because," "although," "while," "if," and "when." To make grammatical sentences, these clauses must be joined to main clauses.

22. FUSED SENTENCES

Do not run sentences together.

Fused sentences are sentences run together with no punctuation or connectors between them. This error may be corrected in four ways:

1. By supplying the appropriate end punctuation between the clauses (period, semicolon, question mark, exclamation point, or colon)

2. By making one of the clauses dependent

3. By inserting a comma and a coordinating conjunction between the clauses, if they are parallel (Inserting only a comma would create a comma splice.)

4. By changing one of the main clauses to a modifying phrase.

1. Fused:

   Most sociology textbooks are poorly written students have trouble deciphering them.

   Corrected by separating the clauses with end punctuation:

Most sociology textbooks are poorly written. Students have trouble deciphering them.

2. Fused:

I'm having trouble in English my professor doesn't appreciate my writing the way my high school teachers did.

Corrected by making the second clause dependent:

I'm having trouble in English because my professor doesn't appreciate my writing the way my high school teachers did.

3. Fused:

I hadn't studied however I went to the movies anyhow.

Corrected by joining the clauses with a comma and a coordinating conjunction:

I hadn't studied, but I went to the movies anyhow.

4. Fused:

My alarm didn't go off therefore I was late.

Corrected by changing the second clause to a modifying phrase:

My alarm didn't go off, making me late.

23. HYPHENS

1. Use a hyphen to join standard compounds such as "twenty-seven," "one-fourth," "sister-in-law," "ex-champion," "self-contained," "author-lecturer."

2. Use a hyphen to join compound adjectives immediately preceding a noun, as in "seventeenth-century writer," "beat-up car," "top-level advisor." When used as other parts of speech, however, such words are not hyphenated:

John Donne lived during the seventeenth century.

Why did he beat up his wife?

Jordan operates at the top level of national politics.

3. Use a hyphen to join certain compound nouns, such as "sit-in," "foul-up," "run-in," "write-in." (Consult your dictionary to be sure.) When used as other parts of speech, however, such words are not hyphenated:

I plan to sit in the sun and relax.

Why did you foul up my plans?

I run in the park for relaxation.

Do not write in the margins.

4. Use a hyphen at the end of a line to divide a word which has to be carried over to the next line. Always divide such words at a syllable break. When in doubt, consult your dictionary, where syllable breaks are indicated by dots: in·ter·rup·tion. Words with prefixes are always divided after the prefix: re-claim, mis-spelling. Never divide a one-syllable word, and never divide a word before or after double letters: er-ror, not e-rror or err-or.

Hold word divisions to a minimum. You are not expected to make the right margins of your papers perfectly even.

5. Use a hyphen in two-word numbers between twenty-one and ninety-nine.

24. IDIOMATIC EXPRESSIONS

Express ideas in natural English.

Idioms are the expressions peculiar to a language. Every language has idioms, and English is filled with them. Because idioms are not governed by the standard rules of logic and grammar, they may be learned only by ear. "Learning by ear" and "playing by ear" are themselves idioms. It would be more logical to say "She can play the piano by hearing," but this expression is unidiomatic. Similarly, something made by hand is really made by hands, but the idiom requires the singular. "This belt is made by hands" and "This belt is handsmade" are unidiomatic sentences. Idioms often do not make literal sense. The expression "centers around" is illogical because a center is in the middle, not around, but "centers around" is idiomatic and "centers in" is not.

Other idioms have nothing to do with figurative language. For instance, the word "according" calls for "to"—as in "according to Hoyle" and "according to informed sources." "According with" won't work simply because it is not the customary expression. On the other hand, we must say "in accordance with," not "in accordance to."

A correct idiom is expressed in a form natural to the language. Expressions such as the following are unidiomatic for the simple reason that they sound wrong to most native speakers of English:

1. Unidiomatic:

A mystical spell has been bound over him.

Idiomatic:

A mystical spell has been cast over him.

Or:

He has been bound by a mystical spell.

2. Unidiomatic:

On the most part, it was a good experience.

Idiomatic:

On the whole, it was a good experience.

Or:

For the most part, it was a good experience.

3. Unidiomatic:

I am escaped by the logic of that statement.

Idiomatic:

The logic of that statement escapes me.

4. Unidiomatic:

Sometimes a person has to stand up with the authorities.

Idiomatic:

Sometimes a person has to stand up to the authorities.

5. Unidiomatic:

We finally narrowed it into two choices.

Idiomatic:

We finally narrowed it down to two choices.

25. INCOMPLETE COMPARISONS

Make both parts of a comparison clear.

Incomplete comparison:

Fitzgerald was more of a romantic. [Than whom?]

Complete comparison:

Fitzgerald was more of a romantic than most of the other American writers of the twenties.

Incomplete comparison:

Debbie was not as well prepared for the test. [As Peggy Sue, as she thought she was, as she was the last time, as she should have been?]

Complete comparison:

Debbie was not as well prepared for the test as she was when she got the highest grade in the class.

Incomplete comparison:

I like college better. [Than high school, than your roommate, than you thought you would, than you did at first?]

Complete comparison:

I like college better than I ever thought I would.

The only time you need not fully state a comparison is when the nature of the comparison is unmistakable from the context or clearly implied by the sentence:

Hemingway was a two-fisted realist. Fitzgerald was more of a romantic.

Peggy Sue made an *A*, but Debbie was not as well prepared.

I had never before seen Harriet so excited.

26. ITALICS

Italics in printing are shown by underlining in typing or handwriting.

1. Underline titles of long works:

> Books: War and Peace, The Rise and Fall of the Third Reich
> Plays: Hamlet, Waiting for Godot
> Extremely long poems: In Memoriam, Beowulf
> Magazines and journals: Time, Southern Humanities Review
> Newspapers: Los Angeles Times, Miami Herald
> Movies: Bonnie and Clyde, Star Wars
> Long musical compositions: Messiah, Swan Lake

Note: Do not underline the titles of your papers.

2. Underline foreign words and phrases:

> Robert likes to think he's a bon vivant.
>
> The military demands esprit de corps.
>
> The modern zeitgeist seems to be apathy and self-absorption.

Note: To avoid the risk of making your readers feel ignorant, use only the most common of such terms. Never use a foreign word or phrase that can't be found in an English dictionary.

Do not underline the many words and phrases

from other languages which are now considered part of English vocabulary. Examples: cafe, vita, boudoir, chalet, coup, fiesta, panache, adobe, papoose, ad hoc, non sequitur, cul de sac, a la carte, carte blanche.

3. Underline words used as words:

Avoid newly coined words such as <u>feedback</u> and <u>remediation</u>.

For some strange reason, <u>lose</u> is commonly misspelled as <u>loose</u>.

Note: Quotation marks may be used instead of underlining for a word used as a word. Whichever you choose, be consistent within the same paper. And never use both underlining and quotation marks for a word.

4. Underline letters used as letters and numbers used as numbers:

A <u>B</u> indicates that you have done above-average work.

I was overdrawn because I transposed a <u>2</u> with a <u>9</u> in my checkbook.

5. Underline for emphasis:

What you say is important, but <u>how</u> you say it is just as crucial.

Melvin not only looked sneaky—he <u>was</u> sneaky.

Note: You must not overuse underlining for emphasis. Once or twice per paper is about the limit. Avoid:

Judy was <u>all right</u>. She was a real <u>beauty</u>, and she also had this <u>fantastic</u> personality.

27. LEGIBILITY

Write clearly.

You are responsible for making your composition readable. If a word cannot be deciphered with reasonable effort, it will be marked illegible. The obvious solution to this problem is to write neatly. If your handwriting is poor and you cannot improve it (most can), then you should print in-class papers and type out-of-class papers. If you have another person type your papers, remember that your typist should do no editing for you and that you are responsible for any errors, typing or otherwise, which appear on the final copy.

28. LOGIC

Avoid unclear or fallacious reasoning.

Many of the logic errors in writing are the result of careless wording rather than fallacious reasoning. These errors, nonetheless, convey the effect of muddled thinking. Take, for instance, this sentence: "She does not want to leave home because she hates her parents." This statement makes no sense because hating one's parents *would* be a reason for wanting to leave home. "She wants to leave home because she hates her parents" makes much more sense. The meaning intended, however, is probably this: "The reason she wants to leave home is not that she hates her parents" (but another reason).

Proofread carefully for sentence sense—especially for contradictions. Nonsense sentences are worse than any grammatical error. The sweeping generalization is such a common error in logic that it has been given a separate section (see p. 359). Also be on guard against these common logical fallacies:

1. Begging the question: embedding within a proposition an unproven statement and treating it as if it required no proof. For example "The un-American activities of anti-nuclear demonstrators must be stopped" states that opposing nuclear power is an un-American activity—a contention which is offered without proof.

2. Post hoc: mistaking a time relationship for cause and effect. Suppose a student has an argument with a professor and eventually ends up with a *D* for the course; the student then concludes that he received the *D* because of the argument. The post hoc fallacy is based upon the erroneous reasoning that since B (the poor grade) followed A (the argument), then B must have been caused by A. But such "reasoning" fails to consider other factors (such as the quality of the student's work) of greater relevance to the cause and effect relationship.

3. Ad hominem: an argument directed "to the man." The ad hominem fallacy takes two forms. One is appealing to the prejudices and self-interest of your audience; the other is attacking the personality and character of your opponent. This example illustrates both: "The president of the college, who everyone knows is a sexually repressed Puritan, has violated our God-given freedom of choice by forbidding pot-smoking in the classroom."

4. Non sequitur: an inference that does not follow from the premises. For instance, "Melanie Cartwright is a great novelist because I really enjoy her writing" is a non sequitur because appeal does not necessarily signify greatness.

5. Circular statement: a statement in which the second part merely repeats the first. For example, "The profit motive inspires big business to seek economic gain" is a circular statement because the idea of seeking economic gain is stated by the term "profit motive."

29. MIXED METAPHORS

Don't mix figures of speech.

The term "mixed metaphor" refers to all types of mixed figures of speech. A figure of speech is an imaginative expression which communicates meaning by a pictorial effect or by analogy—as in "My heart soared like an eagle." In using metaphorical, or figurative, language, be consistent in your terminology. Don't mix images.

Mixed metaphor:

> She used her daughter as a crutch to fall back on. (Crutches aren't used as cushions.)

Improved:

> She used her daughter as a crutch to support her weak will.

Mixed metaphor:

> He wore his humility like a signpost. (Signposts aren't worn.)

Improved:

> He wore his humility like a badge.

Mixed metaphor:

The plan was crippled by a single flaw. (Flaws don't cripple.)

Improved:

The plan was marred by a single flaw.

Mixed metaphor:

The sword of her stubbornness untangled the red tape. (Swords aren't used to untangle.)

Improved:

The sword of her stubbornness slashed through the red tape.

Mixed metaphor:

The reporter doggedly dethroned the corrupt politician. (Dogs don't dethrone.)

Improved:

The reporter doggedly sniffed the trail of corruption until he treed his prey.

30. OMISSIONS

Do not omit necessary words.

Some omissions result in substandard diction: "He is the type person who gets along with everyone" instead of "He is the type *of* person who gets along with everyone." Omissions in certain parallel sentences can create awkwardness: "I didn't want just to compete but win" instead of "I didn't want just to compete but *to* win." The most commonly omitted word is "that":

Wrong:

> Until my father went to college, he didn't know my mother could be so much help to him.

Improved:

> Until my father went to college, he didn't know *that* my mother could be so much help to him.

Wrong:

> James was so handsome he forgot to develop a personality.

Improved:

> James was so handsome *that* he forgot to develop a personality.

Wrong:

> I learned carpentry so I could remodel my house.

Improved:

> I learned carpentry so *that* I could remodel my house.

Compare this "so that" sentence to two main clauses joined by the coordinating conjunction "so":

> I had learned carpentry, so I did my own remodeling.

Omissions result in awkward or ungrammatical sentences which detract from what you have to say. Most of them are caused by hurried composition and lax proofreading. The obvious solution to this problem is to write and proofread as carefully as possible.

31. ORGANIZATION

Stick to the subject and present your ideas in their most logical order.

Organization refers to the overall structure of a piece of writing. An organized paper hangs together in thought. There are many ways to organize essays, but the most workable method is to state the main idea of your paper in an opening paragraph and then devote a separate paragraph in the body to each major division of thought. It is usually a good idea to add a short concluding paragraph which brings the paper to a satisfying close.

You should stick to the subject and include only those ideas which are logically related to your thesis (the main idea of your essay). In addition, you should develop the parts, or major divisions of your paper, in their most logical and effective order. Organization refers to what you include and the order in which you include it. (See Outlining, p. 7, and Organization, p. 14.)

32. PARAGRAPHING

Begin a new paragraph to indicate the divisions of your paper.

When you have completed discussion of one subdivision of your paper and are ready to begin developing the next, begin a new paragraph. In short papers, there is usually one paragraph in the body for each main point, although some points may require two. In longer papers, however, you may find that you need to write several paragraphs to develop each major point adequately. This is usually true of research papers in particular. The general rule is to begin a new paragraph for each major shift in thought. In narratives, shifts in action or locale call for a new paragraph. In dialogue, begin a new paragraph for changes of speaker.

The length of a paragraph in an essay depends, of course, upon how much development its main idea requires. As a general rule, however, both skimpy and lengthy paragraphs should be avoided in most types of writing.

Introductions and conclusions are always set off from the rest of the paper by paragraphing. Never combine an introduction or a conclusion with a paragraph in the body of a paper.

33. PARAGRAPH UNITY

Make all the sentences of a paragraph develop a single idea.

Just as all the paragraphs of a theme should develop a single idea, or thesis, all the sentences of a paragraph should develop one idea, usually stated in a topic sentence at the beginning of the paragraph. Sentences which are off the subject of your paragraph will merely confuse your readers.

Sometimes a paragraph lacking unity may be pulled together by adding transitions to show how the sentences connect. (See Transition within paragraphs, p. 372.) In most cases, however, a paragraph lacks unity simply because some of its sentences do not belong, such as the italicized statements in this example:

Pool is a difficult game. To be good at it, a person

must have steady nerves, unwavering concentration, and superior hand-eye coordination. *Willie Mosconi is one of the best.* A good pool-shooter knows how to be poised and relaxed at the same time. *Although there are high-class poolrooms, called "billiard parlors," in many cities, most people don't consider pool a respectable sport.* In addition to learning to make all the many shots, a pool-player must master English (putting the right spin on the cueball) in order to play position. *There aren't many pool tournaments, and first prize is still in the low thousands. Compare this to the big purses for golf and tennis!* Position—setting up the next shot—is just as important as making the ball. Against a good shooter, a player who can't get position on the next ball may not get to shoot but once. It is not unusual for a cool-headed, experienced player to "run the table" (make all the remaining balls without a miss). The physical and mental control of the pool shark should not be underrated.

Here is the same paragraph unified:

Pool is a difficult game. To be good at it, a person must have steady nerves, unwavering concentration, and superior hand-eye coordination. A good pool-shooter knows how to be poised and relaxed at the same time. In addition to learning to make all the many shots, a pool-player must master English (putting the right spin on the cueball) in order to play position. Position—setting up the next shot—is just as important as making the ball. Against a good shooter, a player who can't get position on the next ball may not get to shoot but once. It is not unusual for a cool-headed, experienced pool-player to "run the table" (make all the remaining balls without a miss). The physical and mental control of the pool shark should not be underrated.

34. PARENTHESES

1. Use parentheses to enclose an explanatory word, phrase, or clause:

> The heavyweight fight matched a classy veteran (Ali) against a brash newcomer (Spinks).
>
> A good linebacker must learn how to blitz (crash through the opposing line).
>
> I didn't speak out for several good reasons (but mainly because I was afraid).

Note that sentence punctuation goes outside parentheses except when the parenthetical comment is a main clause:

> I wanted to make my parents proud of me. (I also wanted to impress my girlfriend.)

This use of parentheses to mark parenthetical material is similar to the use of dashes, but parentheses enclose and dashes set off—a subtle but stylistically important distinction. Material enclosed within parentheses is played down. Material set off by dashes is emphasized. Dashes shout. (Parentheses whisper.) Unlike dashes, parentheses always occur in pairs. Never use parentheses within parentheses, and don't substitute parentheses for brackets.

2. Use parentheses to enclose cross references:

> Don't confuse brackets (see p. 275) with parentheses.

3. Use parentheses to enclose references incorporated into the text of a research paper:

Tennyson's Ulysses vows "To strive, to seek, to find, and not to yield" ("Ulysses," l. 70).

Note that sentence punctuation is placed *after* the parentheses in incorporated references.

35. PERIODS

1. Use a period at the end of a declarative sentence (a sentence which does not ask a question or show unusually strong feeling):

Writing is difficult, but it can be rewarding.

Punctuation seems complicated at first.

He asked what I planned to do. (Note that so-called indirect questions are really statements and therefore end with periods.)

2. Use a period at the end of an imperative (command) sentence which does not show strong feeling:

Turn right at the next stop.

Study hard tonight.

But compare:

Get off my foot!

3. Use a period to mark abbreviations (such as p.m., Dec., M.D., Rev., Va., J. S. Jones, Jr., B.C., vol., Dr., Mrs., Ms., Mr.).

4. Use a period to indicate a fraction (.07, 98.6, 51.2%).

5. Use a period to separate dollars from cents ($0.39, $2.98).

36. PLAGIARISM

The accepted definition of "plagiarism" is "passing off as your own the ideas or words of another writer." This definition covers papers written for you by another student and papers copied from another student. Copying from a book or an article without documenting your source also is plagiarism. In fact, *any unacknowledged use of another person's ideas or wording is plagiarism—even if the idea repeated is only one phrase and even if the other writer's thought is expressed in your own words.*

Changing a word or two or even all the wording of an idea taken from a source does not make the idea your own. Paraphrases (completely reworded and restructured thoughts from sources) must be acknowledged by footnotes. When all or part of an idea taken from a source is quoted word for word, quotation marks around the duplicated words or phrases are required, in addition to a footnote.

Although not expressly stated in the definition of plagiarism, it is also dishonest to have another person edit a paper which you are turning in for a grade. If someone corrects your spelling, punctuation, grammar, or sentence structure, then the paper does not represent just your own work. Most teachers will permit you to have another student read your papers and offer general criticism, but you must do your own correcting and revising.

When you turn in a piece of writing, whether it is a theme or a research paper, you should be able to say, "Except where I have indicated by quotation marks and footnotes, the ideas, wording, style, and mechanics of this paper are my own work." Aside from the fact that plagiarism is dishonest, you cannot learn to write by copying or by having others correct your writing for you. (For specific information on how to handle quotations and paraphrases, see Chapter 3.)

37. PRONOUN AGREEMENT

Match pronouns with their antecedents.

A pronoun (a word substituting for a noun) must agree with its antecedent (the noun to which the pronoun refers) in gender, number, and person.

Gender is masculine, feminine, or neuter. Number is either singular or plural. First-person pronouns (such as "I") refer to the writer or speaker; second-person pronouns ("you," "your," "yours") are used in directly addressing a listener or reader; third-person pronouns (such as "they," "him," and "theirs") refer to the subject being discussed. Follow these rules in troublesome pronoun constructions:

1. A pronoun referring to nouns joined by "and" is plural:

   Flannery O'Connor and Eudora Welty use Southern settings in *their* writing.

   Put up the bicycles and the skateboard so that *they* won't be stolen.

2. A pronoun referring to singular nouns joined by "or," "nor," or the combinations "either . . . or" or "neither . . . nor" is singular:

   Mary or Jane will let you see *her* notes.

   Neither Grandpa nor Freddy would eat *his* cereal.

   When the nouns joined differ in number, the pronoun agrees with the nearer antecedent:

Neither Mr. Hurlbutt nor his students completed *their* assignment.

Neither the students nor Mr. Hurlbutt completed *his* assignment.

This construction is awkward, however, and should be avoided by rewriting:

The students didn't complete the assignment, and neither did Mr. Hurlbutt.

3. Indefinite pronouns such as "each," "either," "neither," "no one," and "everybody" take singular pronouns:

Each of the warriors preserved *his* honor.

Either of the men could lose *his* job.

Neither of the girls liked *her* schedule.

No one on the Rams played *his* best.

Everybody in the sorority did *her* part.

Because of the concern for nonsexist language, these pronouns sometimes cause problems. For instance, "Each of the voters did his duty" may offend some people by the use of "his" to refer to both men and women. The alternative "Each of the voters did his or her duty" is awkward. Probably the best solution is to avoid these troublesome pronouns whenever possible: "All the voters did their duty."

However, due to the trend against sexist language and also to longstanding colloquial usage, sentences such as these are gaining acceptance in written English:

Each of the voters did their duty.

Either of the students will let you see their notes.

Neither of the lions lost their freedom.

No one left their seat until the end.

Everybody in the class did their best.

4. "None" takes a singular or a plural pronoun, depending upon context:

None of the students [plural] failed to complete *their* papers.

None of his work [singular] shows the effort he puts into *it*.

5. a. A collective noun takes a singular pronoun if the group is considered as a unit:

The team reached *its* potential in the last game.

b. A collective noun takes a plural pronoun if it is considered as a collection of individuals:

The battered team dragged *themselves* off the bus and trudged toward *their* cars.

6. Whether a relative pronoun is singular or plural is determined by the number of its antecedent:

Faulkner is one of eight American authors [plural antecedent] *who* received the Nobel Prize in recognition of *their* accomplishments.

Faulkner is an American author [singular antecedent] *who* received the Nobel Prize for *his* novels.

7. Use "who" to refer to people, "which" to refer to things, and "that" to refer to people, things, or animals:

This is the man *who* saved my life.

Rules *which* don't make sense should be changed.

The person *that* I'm referring to is not here.

There is the dog *that* has been digging up my flowers.

This type of sentence, however, is ungrammatical:

Mr. Garp, that is my chemistry teacher, is an avid jogger.

Correct:

Mr. Garp, *who* is my chemistry teacher, is an avid jogger.

8. Don't shift from "I" to "you" without a purpose.

Incorrect:

I wondered what you were supposed to do in a situation like that.

Correct:

I wondered what *I* [or a person] was supposed to do in a situation like that.

38. PRONOUN CASE

Use the correct pronoun form for nominative, objective, and possessive cases.

Pronouns in the *nominative* case function as subjects. The nominative pronoun forms are "I," "we," "he," "she," "they," and "who."

Pronouns in the *objective* case function as the object of verbs ("Jeff hit *him*"), of prepositions ("To *whom* are you speaking?"), of verbals ("Fighting *them* is no fun"), and as "subjects" of infinitives ("I wanted *her* to win"). The objective pronoun forms are "me," "us," "him," "her," "them," and "whom." "You" may be either nominative or objective. ("You are the one; I want you.")

Pronouns in the *possessive* case indicate ownership. The possessive pronouns are "my"/"mine," "our"/"ours," "your"/"yours," "their"/"theirs," "her"/"hers," "his," and "its." Note: Do not use apostrophes with possessive pronouns, and do not confuse the possessive "its" with "it's," the contraction of "it is."

Pronoun case is troublesome in these constructions:

1. Compound objects

   He spoke to Bill and me. (Not "to Bill and I.")

   They thanked Hilda and me. (Not "Hilda and I.")

   In sentences with compound, or double, objects, you can arrive at the correct pronoun form by mentally eliminating the other object. If you eliminate "Bill" from "He spoke to Bill and I," for instance, "He spoke to I" is easily detected as incorrect.

2. Comparisons

   John is smarter than he. (Not "John is smarter than him.")

   Such constructions are elliptical, or shortened, sentences:

   John is smarter than he [is].

   In comparisons, mentally repeat the verb to arrive at the correct pronoun form.

3. Who/whom clauses
   a. The nominative "who" is required when the pronoun functions as the subject of a clause:

      John, *who dropped out of school,* joined the army.

      Mary is the one person *who could win.*

In such sentences, "who" functions as the subject of the clause by substituting for the real subject:

> [John] dropped out of school.
>
> [One person, Mary,] could win.

b. The objective form "whom" is required when the pronoun functions as an object:

> Mary is the person *whom you want to contact.* ("You want to contact *whom.*")

This sentence, however, would normally be shortened to "Mary is the person you want to contact."

"Whom" has virtually passed out of usage except when it immediately follows a preposition:

> To *whom* do you wish to speak?
>
> For *whom* have you done this?

4. Pronouns with gerunds (nouns made by adding "-ing" to verbs)

> I did not appreciate *his* [not "him"] criticizing me.

In this construction, "his" modifies the noun "criticizing." Objective-case pronouns (such as "him") cannot function as modifiers. Gerunds such as "criticizing" may look like verbs, but they function as nouns. Compare: I did not appreciate *his* criticism of me.

39. PRONOUN REFERENCE

Make pronoun references clear and grammatical.

A pronoun must be preceded by an antecedent which clearly identifies the pronoun and agrees with it in person, number, and gender. Pronoun antecedents may be nouns, noun clauses, gerunds (nouns made by adding "-ing" to a verb), or infinitives (nouns made up of "to" plus a verb):

Fred [noun] was outclassed, and *he* knew it.

That Fred was outclassed [noun clause] was obvious, and *it* made him play worse than ever.

Writing [gerund] is difficult, but I like *it*.

I like to write [infinitive], but *it* is hard work.

There are four basic pronoun reference errors:

1. Pronoun with no antecedent. A pronoun lacking an antecedent is almost always the result of carelessness:

   Andrew lost his job bagging groceries because he was constantly being rude to *them* [no antecedent].

   Joe planned to study all night for the test because *it* [no antecedent] was a subject he was failing.

   Technically, a pronoun lacks an antecedent (which means a noun or noun form "coming before") if the "antecedent" is placed *after* the pronoun:

   For *her* debut, *Courtney* chose a purple gown.

   Despite *his* early death, *Keats* produced many great poems.

   Revisions:

   Courtney chose a purple gown for *her* debut.

   Keats, despite *his* early death, produced many great poems.

   Do not begin paragraphs with pronouns. Even though the reference of a pronoun beginning a paragraph may be clear from the preceding paragraph, such a pronoun technically lacks an antecedent. The noun referred to by a pronoun should immediately precede the pronoun in the *same* paragraph. It is bad style to use pronouns to refer back across paragraph breaks to antecedents.

2. Pronoun with hidden antecedent

   a. Pronoun separated from antecedent by intervening nouns:

      Math has always been hard for me. English is my best subject, but *it* is bringing my average down.

      The nouns "subject" and "English" separate "it" from its antecedent "Math," causing unnecessary confusion.

      Place antecedents as close to pronouns as possible. When such placement would create an awkward sentence, revise the sentence to eliminate the unclear pronoun:

      English is my best subject, but math, which has always been hard for me, is bringing my average down.

   b. Ambiguous reference—pronoun with two possible antecedents:

      When Paul worked for the governor, *he* [Paul or the governor?] was always in trouble with the press.

      Revisions:

      Paul was always in trouble with the press when he worked for the governor.

Or:

> The governor was always in trouble with the press when Paul worked for him.

3. Pronoun with vague antecedent (generalized reference)

> Mary quit her low-paying job as a waitress when her employer continued to insult her. *This* was what she wanted to escape.

(Does "this" refer to continuous insults, difficult employer, low-paying job, or all three?)

Revision:

> Mary quit her low-paying job when her employer continued to insult her. She wanted to escape her wretched existence as a waitress.

Or:

> Mary quit her low-paying job as a waitress when her employer continued to insult her. She wanted to escape this abuse.

Vague reference often results from the pronoun "this." In proofreading, make sure that all "this" pronouns have clear antecedents.

4. Pronoun with ungrammatical antecedent

a. An antecedent cannot be a possessive noun:

> In *John's* haste, *he* forgot the tickets.

Revision:

> *John,* in *his* haste, forgot the tickets.

b. An antecedent cannot be an appositive:

"A Rose for Emily," by William Faulkner, is one of *his* most famous short stories.

Revision:

"A Rose for Emily" is one of William Faulkner's most famous short stories.

c. An antecedent cannot be a noun used as an adjective:

There is more to being a good *volleyball* player than spiking it.

Revision:

There is more to being a good volleyball player than spiking the ball.

To test the grammatical correctness of pronoun reference, see if the antecedent will substitute for the pronoun in the sentence. Example:

Almost everyone wants *to be needed*. Without *it*, many people can't survive.

Substitution:

Almost everyone wants to be needed. Without [to be needed], many people can't survive. (Incorrect)

Revision:

Being needed is important to most people. Without [being needed], many people can't survive.

Note: Do not confuse the pronoun "it" with the expletive "it" in such sentences as "It is raining" and "It is up to you to decide." Expletives do not take antecedents.

Avoid the awkward pronoun plus antecedent-in-parentheses construction:

After *John* and his father discussed the scheme, *he (John)* decided not to pursue it.

Revision:

John, after discussing the scheme with *his* father, decided not to pursue it.

40. QUESTION MARKS

1. Use a question mark after sentences which ask for information and require a direct response:

> Who was that?
>
> Are you speaking to me?
>
> Did John win?
>
> What is the capital of North Dakota?
>
> How do you spell "develop"?
>
> "Where's the toothbrush?" asked Father.

2. Use a question mark after rhetorical questions:

> What did Sammy do then? Well, he picked up his marbles and went home.
>
> How can young writers learn to use fresh language when their idols speak in slogans and clichés?

> Convention requires that such rhetorical questions be followed by a question mark, although they are not really questions. Rhetorical questions are not designed to receive an answer but to make a point or set up a statement. Use them sparingly.

3. *Do not* use a question mark after sentences which are worded as questions but are really commands or exclamations:

Do you want to step over here please.

Will you shut the door.

Will you people get back in line!

Well, who would have thought!

Note that such sentences do not have the rise in voice at the end which is characteristic of genuine questions.

4. *Do not* use a question mark after indirect questions:

Todd wanted to know where I went on my vacation.

Brian asked if he could be excused.

An indirect question is not really a question at all but a declarative statement about a question. Compare the form and inflection of these real questions:

"Where did you go on your vacation?" Todd wanted to know.

Brian asked, "May I be excused?"

41. QUOTATION MARKS

1. Single quotation marks ("   ")

a. Use single quotation marks to enclose titles of short works:

Poems: "The Charge of the Light Brigade"

Short stories: "The Secret Life of Walter Mitty"

Articles: "Tennyson as Modern Poet" appears in *Critical Essays on the Poetry of Tennyson.*

Chapter headings: For further information, see "Revolt Among the Artists," Chapter II of *The Pre-Raphaelite Poets.*

Songs: "God Bless America"

Paintings: "American Gothic"

Television shows: "The Tonight Show"

Note: Do not put quotation marks around the titles of your papers.

b. Use single quotations marks to enclose direct quotations of all types:

Virgil smiled at me and said, "Now don't that beat all!"

Hartsell's favorite saying was "Do unto others before they do unto you."

Of *In Memoriam*, T. S. Eliot wrote, "Its faith is a poor thing, but its doubt is a very intense experience."

In Tennyson's "The Eagle," the images "crooked hands," "wrinkled sea," and "thunderbolt" are very effective.

In "The Love Song of J. Alfred Prufrock," Prufrock says, "I have measured out my life with coffee spoons."

In *The Sandbox*, Grandma complains, "What a way to treat an old woman!"

Note: Poetry quotations of four lines or more and prose quotations which run five lines or more in your paper should be indented (blocked). Quotation marks are *not* used with indented quotations unless quotation marks already appear in the original passage.

c. Use single quotation marks to indicate words used as words:

The words "ongoing" and "input" are perversions of the English language.

Don't call me "babe"!

Note: Italics (underlining) may be used instead of quotation marks for a word used as a word. Whichever device you choose, be consistent within the same paper. Never underline a word and also put it in quotation marks.

d. Use single quotation marks to emphasize that an expression is used sarcastically or satirically:

With "friends" like Schwartz, who needs enemies?

The main reference source of this "scholar" is *Harry's Quik Notes.*

A "man for all seasons," Reggie cuts class to play in good weather and bad.

e. Use single quotation marks to indicate the intentional use of a slang or colloquial expression:

Never use a thesaurus to "fancy up" your writing.

A smart consumer never buys "a pig in a poke."

If you don't watch out when you "hang ten," you'll end up in traction.

Strategically used, such expressions can be effective. They should not, however, be overdone, as in this example:

He thinks he's a "cool dude" because he gets "stoned" on "pot" every night.

f. Use single quotation marks to indicate "interior dialogue" and hypothetical quotations (usually questions):

> I thought to myself, "If only I could get to the telephone!"

> The big question is "How can I pass English without going to class?"

2. Double quotation marks (" '   ' ")
   a. Use double quotation marks to enclose material which already is quoted in the original source (thus making a quotation within a quotation):

   > According to John Killham, Alfred Noyes said that "there were really two Tennysons—'the black unhappy mystic of the Lincolnshire wolds' and 'the prosperous Isle-of-Wight Victorian.'"

   b. Use double quotation marks when a title requiring quotation marks is part of a longer title also requiring quotation marks:

   > I'm working on an article entitled "Military Strategy in 'The Charge of the Light Brigade.'"

3. Punctuation with quotation marks
   a. Question marks may go either inside or outside the closing quotation mark, depending upon the sentence. If the quotation itself is a question, the question mark goes inside the quotation mark:

   > Tamico asked, "Aren't you being unfair?"

   If the entire sentence is a question, the question mark goes outside the quotation mark:

Who said "Give me liberty or give me death"?

b. Exclamation points may go either inside or outside the closing quotation mark, depending upon the sentence. If the quotation itself is an exclamation, the exclamation point goes inside the quotation mark:

"Shut up!" he bellowed.

If the entire sentence is an exclamation, the exclamation point goes outside the quotation mark:

"Gripe, gripe, gripe" is all you ever do!

c. Commas and periods after quotations or titles always go *inside* the closing quotation mark:

By "Do not go gentle into that good night," Dylan Thomas means that everyone should fight against death.

In "To His Coy Mistress," a young cavalier attempts to seduce his lady fair.

Some people think stealing is justified if they call it "ripping off."

One of Robert Frost's best-known poems is "After Apple-Picking."

d. Semicolons and colons always go *outside* quotation marks:

Marvell's young cavalier laments, "had we but world enough, and time"; however, he is merely setting the stage for seduction.

One of Marvell's most famous couplets is in "To His Coy Mistress": "But at my back I always hear / Time's wingèd chariot hurrying near."

42. REPETITIOUS SENTENCE STRUCTURE

**Avoid repetitious sentence structure
by varying sentence style.
Don't string together short clauses.**

1. Repetitious sentence structure usually is created by short clauses cast in a monotonous sequence of subject-verb-complement sentences. (A complement completes the meaning of the verb.) Example:

> The radicals of the late sixties did some good. They had an impact on campus values. They helped change clothing and hair styles. They helped create some new courses of study. They inspired environmental studies. They promoted more learning-by-doing. Some of this now takes place in off-campus jobs. Some of these jobs are related to the student's major.

Don't attempt to eliminate repetitious sentence structure by merely stringing together main clauses. Combining short sentences into longer ones has not improved style in the following paragraph:

> The radicals of the late sixties did some good. They helped change clothing and hair styles, and they inspired some new courses of study, and one of these was environmental studies. They promoted more learning-by-doing, and some of this now takes place in off-campus jobs, and some of these jobs are related to the student's major.

To achieve sentence variety, combine related ideas by using subordination (see p. 358) and coordination (see p. 291):

Modern college students are indebted to the radicals of the sixties for many of the freedoms they now enjoy. Mainly because of the impact of these rebels on campus values, students can now dress and wear their hair the way they please. The sixties' cry for relevance has left a legacy of valid new courses, such as environmental studies, and more learning-by-doing in off-campus jobs related to the student's major.

2. Overuse of similar phrases and dependent clauses within the same sentence also causes repetitious sentence structure. Example:

> The man featured in the business section in today's newspaper is my father, who is a builder who lives in Virginia.

Improved:

> The man featured in the business section of today's newspaper is my father, who is a builder in Virginia.

43. SEMICOLONS

1. Use a semicolon to separate items in a series which contains several commas:

> The following people are on the Board of Trustees: Cy Ryan, a politician; Rachel Springs, a newspaper publisher; S. T. Tuggleman, a banker; Henry Poltiss, a physician; Nan Booker, a student.

Except for such lists, a useful rule for semicolons is: *Use semicolons only where a period would be correct.*

2. You may use a semicolon to separate two closely related, parallel sentences:

Fred attended college for six years; nevertheless, he did not graduate.

When I was younger, I thought nothing could stop me; now that I'm older, I know better.

The semicolon may be thought of as a "weak period": Like the period, it separates sentences; unlike the period, it signifies a very close relationship between the sentences it "separates." Grammatically, the semicolon is "stop" punctuation like the period and not "pause" punctuation like the comma. Nevertheless, it really joins ideas more than it separates them. The semicolon separates main clauses grammatically, but it joins them rhetorically:

Harry brought the hot dogs; Bess brought the beer; Herman brought himself.

Like any rhetorical device, semicolon sentences lose their effectiveness if they are overused. Use the semicolon sparingly between parallel main clauses not joined by coordinating conjunctions; never use it in place of a colon after an introductory statement; use it in place of a comma only in the special case of long lists with commas.

44. SPELLING

Like many other things, good spelling is easy for some and hard for others. Some very intelligent people (Scott Fitzgerald, for instance) have been notoriously bad spellers. Poor spelling nonetheless detracts from writing; and, unlike Fitzgerald, most people don't have editors to correct their spelling for them.

Poor spelling is one of the most difficult writing problems to remedy because there are as many chances for error as there are words in your paper. Learning to spell is largely a process of memorization. Spelling correctly, however, is simply a matter of taking the time to use your dictionary. On in-class papers, look up as many doubtfully spelled words as you can *after* your paper is written. If you stop repeatedly to look up words while writing the paper, you probably won't finish it. On out-of-class papers, you should look up *all* the words you aren't sure of. (Buy an unabridged dictionary. Many of the words you'll need to find won't be in an abridged dictionary.)

A common error in dictionary use is to mistake the dot in such words as "half·back" as designating two words. Such dots show syllable division *within* words, not separation between words ("halfback"). If word pairs should be written separately, they will appear in the dictionary with no dividing mark between them (example: "all right"). Only a few commonly paired words, however, are listed in dictionaries.

If you fail to locate a two-word construction in an unabridged dictionary, it almost certainly is not a compound and therefore should be written as two separate words. The exception to this principle is compound adjectives, such as "two-word" in the previous sentence, which are always hyphenated. Most of these constructions aren't listed in dictionaries.

The fact that a spelling is given in a dictionary does not always mean that the spelling is appropriate. The construction "alright," for instance, is listed in the *American Heritage Dictionary,* but it is described as "a common misspelling." Obviously, the correct version of such constructions should be used.

There are.so many exceptions to the few rules which have been devised for English spelling that these rules are virtually useless. Besides, in the time it takes to recall a rule and determine whether it applies, you can look up the word in your dictionary. The only spelling rule worth remembering is that the final *e* on practically all words is dropped before adding -*ing:* believing, boring, lunging, hoping, loving, leaving.

Here is an abbreviated list of some of the most commonly misspelled words:

a lot (misspelled as "alot")

category

definite

develop

disappoint

disastrous

dissatisfied

embarrass

environment

exaggerate

excel

existence

forty

fulfill

hindrance

it's (contraction of "it is")

its (possessive pronoun)

loneliness

lose (misspelled as "loose")

occasion

occurrence

optimism

parallel

perform

possess

precede

prejudiced

prerogative

privilege

proceed

receive

repetitious

separate

succeed

tendency

their (for expletive "there")

to (for "too")

tragedy

truly

undoubtedly

villain

weird

The key to correct spelling may be stated in three words: Use your dictionary.

45. SUBJECT-VERB AGREEMENT

Verbs must agree with their subjects in person and number. Most native writers and speakers automatically make subjects and verbs agree simply because of cultural conditioning. Most people, for instance, don't instinctively write or say "I studies" or "He work hard." Those who do use such constructions benefit little from the information that the verb "studies" is third-person singular and that the verb "work" can be either third-person plural or first-person singular.

Subject-verb agreement is learned primarily by unconscious imitation of the speakers we hear and the writers we read, not by rote memorization. The following rules, however, will aid you in proofreading for subject-verb agreement in especially troublesome constructions:

1. Subjects joined by "and" require a plural verb:

   The Johnson sisters and their cousin Bill *are* graduating next year.

   English, math, and biology *give* me trouble.

2. Singular subjects connected by "or," "nor," or the combinations "either . . . or" or "neither . . . nor" take singular verbs:

   Brown or Simpson *is* available.

   Neither Brown nor Simpson *is* available.

3. Plural subjects joined by "or," "nor," or the combinations "either . . . or" or "neither . . . nor" take plural verbs:

   Department chairmen or their representatives *are* expected to attend.

Either unexcused absences or late papers *affect* your grade.

4. When subjects differing in number are joined by "or," "nor," or the combinations "either . . . or" or "neither . . . nor," the verb agrees with the nearer subject:

Neither the doctor nor the nurses were in.

Neither the nurses nor the doctor was in.

This rather awkward construction, however, may be easily avoided:

The doctor and the nurses were out.

5. Indefinite pronouns such as "each," "either," and "neither" take singular verbs:

Each of you *does* good work.

We must choose between Smith and Brown. Either *is* a good man for the job.

Don't write your research paper on abortion or drug abuse. Neither *is* a fresh topic.

6. Singular subjects followed by such constructions as "including," "in addition to," and "as well as" take singular verbs in spite of their plural effect:

John, as well as his sister, is under psychiatric care.

The construction "as well as his sister" is enclosed by commas to indicate that it is a "sentence interrupter" and not part of a compound subject. The subject is the singular noun "John."

7. "None" takes a singular or a plural verb, depending upon meaning:

None of my trouble [singular] is your fault.

None of the problems [plural] are difficult.

8. Verbs agree with their subjects and not with their subjective complements:

My greatest joy [singular subject] in college *was* the papers [subjective complement] I wrote.

The papers [plural subject] I wrote in college *were* my greatest job [subjective complement].

9. When the subject is a relative pronoun, its verb agrees with the pronoun's antecedent:

Charles is one of those *people* who *are* always critical of others.

"Who," the subject of the relative clause, substitutes for its antecedent "people" and therefore requires a plural verb. The correct form may be arrived at by mentally eliminating the relative pronoun:

"People . . . *are* always critical of others."

The same principle governs a relative pronoun with a singular antecedent:

Charles is the type of *person* who *is* always critical of others.

("A person . . . *is* always critical of others.")

10. A collective noun takes a singular verb when it denotes a unit and a plural verb when it refers to a group considered as individuals:

Our team *works* hard.

My family *don't* get along with one another.

The trend, however, is to treat all collective nouns as singular:

The faculty works hard.

My family doesn't get along.

11. When a sentence is introduced by the expletive "There," the verb agrees with the subject following the verb:

There *are* too many people [plural subject] in this room. (Too many people are in this room.)

There *is* so much noise [singular subject] that I can't think. (So much noise exists that I can't think.)

12. Verbs agree with their subjects and not with intervening nouns:

The last [singular subject] of the late-night movies *was* almost over when the telephone rang.

Manual work [singular subject] such as stone masonry and finish carpentry *is* as much an art as a skill.

13. Numbers used to indicate a singular sum or unit take singular verbs:

Eight years *is* a long time to be in college.

Ten dollars *is* too much for that gadget.

Seventy yards *is* a long run.

14. Nouns which are plural in form but singular in meaning take singular verbs:

Economics *is* a complicated subject.

It has been said that politics *is* the art of compromise.

15. A few nouns which are plural in form may be treated as either singular or plural:

Your writing mechanics (*is* or *are*) improving.

The data (*has* or *have*) been gathered.

Dictionaries usually designate such words as "singular or plural in construction."

46. SUBORDINATION

Express ideas of lesser importance in a single word, a phrase, or a subordinate clause.

1. Subordination needed:

Bill bought a new car. It is a compact.

Revision:

Bill bought a new compact car.

Subordination needed:

Mary has a lot of money. It is in the bank.

Revision:

Mary has a lot of money in the bank.

Subordination needed:

I didn't study, and I failed the test.

Revision:

I failed the test because I didn't study.

Note that the main idea is given even more emphasis

when it is placed in the last part (the "emphatic position") of the sentence:

Because I didn't study, I failed the test.

2. Faulty subordination:

Terry Samms, who just won the Irish Sweepstakes, works in a bank.

This sentence gives more emphasis to Terry's job than it does to the fact that Terry just won a lot of money. A more logical statement would subordinate the job and emphasize the good luck:

Terry Samms, who works in a bank, just won the Irish Sweepstakes.

State important ideas in main clauses, and subordinate lesser ideas.

47. SWEEPING GENERALIZATIONS

Sweeping generalizations are statements which are inaccurate because they are too broad. Avoid them by careful wording or by adding qualifying terms such as "some," "many," "most," "usually," and "sometimes." Sweeping generalizations come in three forms:

1. An extreme statement which is generally—but not always—true:

A college education will give you a comfortable life.

Revision:

A college education *can* give you a comfortable life.

Extreme statement:

These days, everything you buy is higher than it used to be.

Revision:

These days, *almost* everything you buy is higher than it used to be.

2. An extreme statement to which there are many exceptions:

All politicians are just out for themselves.

Revision:

Some politicians are just out for themselves.

Extreme statement:

If you set a goal and work hard, you're sure to achieve it.

Revision:

If you set a goal and work hard, you *have a good chance* of achieving it.

3. A broad conclusion based upon insufficient evidence:

Three of my friends have gotten divorces. This shows that marriage is a dying institution.

Revision:

Divorce has become so common that it now seems to be just a normal part of American life. According to recent figures, almost half of American marriages are ending in divorce. Even among my few married friends, three have already split up with their husbands. The institution of marriage is in trouble.

48. TENSE SHIFTS

Do not shift tenses without a purpose.

Verb tenses establish the time of an action or situation. You should not change tenses unless there is a logical reason for doing so. The three basic tenses are past, present, and future, but there are variations of each:

1. Past:

> We studied. (The past tense of most English verbs is formed by adding "-ed.")

Past perfect:

> We had studied before going to the movie. (Denotes action completed in the past before other past action; formed by "had" + past participle.)

Past progressive:

> We were studying. (Denotes continuing action in the past; formed by past auxiliary of "be" + main verb + "-ing.")

Note: The subjunctive mood, used to express a contrary-to-fact condition, demands a special use of the verb "were," which ordinarily denotes past tense:

> If he were better informed, he would vote against the proposal.

> If I were you, I wouldn't go.

2. Present:

> We study.

Present perfect:

> We have studied. (Denotes past action extending indefinitely to the present; formed by "have" + past participle.)

Present progressive:

> We are studying. (Denotes action continuing in the present; formed by present auxiliary of "be" + main verb + "-ing.")

3. Future:

> We will study. (Denotes action planned for the future; formed by future auxiliary + present tense of main verb.)

Note: There are several idiomatic forms of the future tense, such as "We are going to study" and "We plan to study."

Future perfect:

> By midnight Thursday, we will have studied three days. (Denotes action to be completed at a specific time in the future; formed by "will have" + past participle.)

Most papers are written in the same set of tenses. In certain instances, however, it is incorrect *not* to shift tenses. Such shifts are governed by logic, and the reason for shifting should be clear from the context. Example:

> We studied hard for that history test. In fact, we were slaving away when Weed came by and invited us to a party. "Don't let me down, bookworms," he taunted. Since we had worked for six hours straight, we decided to go. "I will study the Boer War no more," Gene announced, as he slammed shut his book.

This passage has a variety of tenses. Note, however, that except for the dialogue, all tenses are some form of the past.

Less commonly, a writer may shift between present and past tense. Such dramatic tense shifts require clear signals. Example:

Racial strife in America seems to be [present] a way of life. Most of us remember [present] the riots that occurred [past] in the sixties [time designation to clarify shift to past tense]. Even today [signal of shift back into present time], the dispute over busing continues [present].

Most erroneous shifts in tense are the result of carelessness rather than intent. These mistakes should be detected during proofreading. The simple rule governing tense is to stay in the same tense throughout a paper unless there is a compelling reason to shift. When you do have to shift into a different tense, be sure to go back into the dominant tense of the paper after the shift has served its purpose.

Tenses in literary analysis

Literary analysis presents a special problem because of the convention which demands that the "action" of literature be discussed in present-tense verbs. Inexperienced students of literature are prone to use past-tense verbs in literary analysis, probably because they read the selection in the past or because it was written in the past. These facts, however, are irrelevant to the two *present* concerns of explication: "What *is* happening in a work of literature?" and "How *is* its meaning communicated to the reader?"

The principle of discussing literature in present-tense verbs does not apply to historical comments which may be interwoven with analysis. The following passage illustrates the combination of historical past and literary present tenses:

> The Renaissance was [historical past] a time of intense artistic endeavor. Shakespeare wrote [historical/ biographical past] his plays during this period. *Macbeth*, written in 1606, is [literary present] one of his greatest works. In the protagonist, Macbeth, Shakespeare depicts [literary present] the classic tragic figure. Macbeth is [literary present] a good and noble man except for his one weakness: He has [literary present] too much prideful ambition. In Macbeth, Shakespeare gave [historical past] the world one of its most memorable dramatic creations.

The only instance in which simple past tense is correct in referring to plot details is in the special case of antecedent action—action which took place before the opening of the story:

> Nick Adams recalls how his father, who eventually *committed* suicide, *taught* him to hunt and to love the outdoors.

These tense conventions apply to analysis of poetry, fiction, drama, motion pictures, and other art forms.

49. THESIS STATEMENTS

Clearly state the controlling idea of your paper.

The thesis of a paper is a clear and succinct statement of its main idea. The thesis statement should appear in the introductory paragraph and leave no doubt as to exactly what idea the paper will develop.

A paper should have only one thesis statement. Introductory paragraphs with several statements which *could* be the paper's main idea only confuse the reader.

1. Introductory paragraph lacking a thesis statement:

> Although some components of the Ph.D., or Doctor of Philosophy degree, have been criticized as irrelevant, it remains the most prestigious degree offered by colleges and universities throughout the world. Thousands are now enrolled in doctoral programs in the United States. Thirty-two percent of my college graduating class went on to graduate school. I hope to complete another degree someday, but right now I'm happy with my job. I teach junior high English.

This chatty paragraph is composed of details loosely related to the topic of graduate study, but it lacks a clear statement of purpose. It is obvious from the loose generalities that the writer has not planned the paper and doesn't know exactly what it is intended to communicate. Such beginnings almost always result in poorly organized writing.

2. Introductory paragraph with several possible thesis statements:

> Although some components of the Ph.D., or Doctor of Philosophy degree, have been criticized as irrelevant, it remains the most prestigious degree offered by colleges and universities throughout the world. One reason for the prestige of the degree is that it usually requires the completion of a difficult three-step process. There are currently many unemployed Ph.D.'s. Some people go to graduate school for the wrong reasons.

Any one of the last three sentences could be a thesis statement. The writer must decide which one to develop, eliminate the other two, and slant the lead to fit the thesis selected.

3. Introductory paragraph with a clear thesis statement:

> Although some components of the Ph.D., or Doctor of Philosophy degree, have been criticized as irrelevant, it remains the most prestigious degree offered by colleges and universities throughout the world [lead]. One reason for the prestige of the degree is that it requires the completion of a difficult three-step process [thesis statement].

Note the simplicity of this paragraph. After the lead sentence, the writer clearly indicates that the paper will demonstrate one reason for the prestige of the Ph.D. degree by analyzing the three-step process that the candidate must complete. Note also that the broad structure of the essay is suggested in the thesis statement: The reader can reasonably expect a three-part body, one part on each step of the process.

A thesis statement should express the main idea of your paper in a succinct, natural manner. Avoid such expressions as "The purpose of this paper is" and "In this paper, I will."

Thesis statements in literary analysis

Instead of stating a critical or interpretive idea to be proved or demonstrated, students sometimes offer a mere plot detail as their "thesis statement." Since plot details are unarguable facts, such statements leave nothing to develop, as illustrated by this example:

> Many of E. A. Robinson's poems warn against the dehumanizing effects of materialism [lead]. In "The Mill," a miller and his wife commit suicide [thesis].

The supposed thesis, "In 'The Mill,' a miller and his wife commit suicide," is clear enough, but the information it conveys requires no proof, so it permits no development. Moreover, the sentence suggests nothing about either the technique or meaning of the poem. It is a dead end. Instead of giving a plot detail—even the main plot detail—the thesis of a literary analysis must state an idea concerning an important feature or the basic meaning (theme) of the work of literature.

The last sentence of the following introduction is a genuine thesis because it requires development and gives the paper direction:

> Many of E. A. Robinson's poems warn against the dehumanizing effects of materialism. In "The Mill," a brief narrative poem, the villain is technology, the servant of materialism. *The poem depicts the human tragedy which can result when a person is deprived of the dignity of labor.*

This thesis statement demands that the writer supply evidence of a cause-effect relationship between the suicide of the miller and his wife and the fact that technology has made millers obsolete. Development of this thesis would require the writer to use such elements as plot details, tone, and imagery to reveal the underlying meaning of the poem. In short, the thesis directs the writer to *analyze* the poem and not just retell the story.

If a topic is assigned for a literary analysis, simply

convert it into a thesis statement. Suppose that your assignment is to "analyze imagery in 'The Mill.'" Your thesis statement might be "Most of the imagery of 'The Mill' is somber in order to foreshadow the suicide of the miller and his wife, but it shifts from gloomy to serene after their deaths."

If the topic is open (for instance, "Write a critical paper on 'The Mill'"), then formulate a thesis based upon what you consider an outstanding feature or the main idea of the work. Such a thesis may concentrate upon tone, imagery, symbolism, conflict, point of view, analysis of a major character, or how theme is developed. The important thing is that your thesis be a critical idea and not a plot statement.

50. TOPIC SENTENCES

Clearly state the main idea of each paragraph.

A topic sentence is to a paragraph what a thesis statement is to the whole paper. Just as a thesis statement communicates the main idea of a paper, a topic sentence states the main idea of a paragraph. The topic sentence is the most important sentence in a paragraph. It must be especially clear and precise, and it should contain only one major idea. Except for introductions and conclusions, each paragraph in a theme should have a topic sentence.

Sometimes a paragraph will lead up to a topic sentence which is stated last, but the most effective method is to state the topic sentence first in the paragraph. Beginning each paragraph in the body of an essay with a topic sentence has two advantages: (1) It tells your readers what will be covered in the paragraph, thus helping them follow your line of thought, and (2) it forces you to get the main idea of the paragraph clear in your own mind before attempting to develop it.

Do not write development paragraphs without topic sentences, and do not begin paragraphs with misleading topic sentences.

1. Paragraph lacking a topic sentence:

> The news media have played up the idea that today's college students are the most illiterate ever. Public clamor continues over the steady decline of SAT verbal scores during recent years. Many educators have jumped on this bandwagon of despair. Some of the nation's top schools, such as the University of California at Berkeley, have begun remedial English programs. Most of the English professors interviewed in articles and on television documentaries seem to think their students used to write better. These test scores and opinions may not be right.

Because this paragraph lacks a topic sentence to unify its details, readers may be left wondering what the writer is driving at. The last sentence shifts gears completely, from a gloomy picture of current literacy to the idea that it may not be so bad after all. Those readers who take the first sentence to be the topic sentence may be puzzled when they find that the paragraph deals with much more than the role of the news media.

2. Paragraph with a misleading topic sentence:

> Learning to write well is a challenge. The news media have played up the idea that today's college students are the most illiterate ever. Public clamor continues over the steady decline of SAT verbal scores during recent years. Many educators have jumped on

this bandwagon of despair. Some of the nation's top schools, such as the University of California at Berkeley, have begun remedial English programs. Most of the English professors interviewed in articles and on television documentaries seem to think their students used to write better. These test scores and opinions may not be right.

The topic sentence of this paragraph is misleading because there is nothing in the paragraph on the challenge of learning to write well.

3. The same paragraph with a topic sentence to give it direction and coherence:

There is no conclusive evidence that today's college students write worse than those of the past. The news media have played up the idea that contemporary college students are the most illiterate ever, possibly creating a crisis where none exists. Responding to this bad press and to the public clamor over the steady decline of SAT verbal scores during recent years, many educators have jumped on this bandwagon of despair. Some of the nation's top schools, such as the University of California at Berkeley, have begun remedial English programs. But do SAT scores really mean anything? Until recently, the test was entirely objective, a doubtful indicator of writing ability or functional literacy. The current test includes a short essay, but its objective part is still weighted heavily in the total score. It is also possible that the English professors who say their students used to write better are victims of nostalgia. The old days tend to become the "good ol' days," and they may just *think* their students used to be better. Objective test scores and memory form a shaky basis for the charge that today's college students are verbal dunces.

Topic sentences in literary analysis

Probably because of the difficulty of breaking down a unified work of art into main points, there is a tendency in literary analysis to begin paragraphs with plot details rather than topic sentences. Because the following paragraph begins with such a detail (in this case, a quotation), the reader must read the entire paragraph and *then* attempt to deduce the point the writer wants to make. Don't expect your readers to do this much work for you.

Paragraph with plot detail for topic sentence:

> The duke says, "E'en then would be some stooping; and I choose / Never to stoop." It is pathetically ironic that the duke never mentioned his unhappiness to his bride. The duke could not forgive his wife for not sharing his pride in his position. "She had / A heart," he says, "too soon made glad." The duchess seems to have had no sense of social superiority, a dangerously liberal attitude for one married to a man obsessed with his birth and position.

Converting the quotation into a paraphrase, such as "The duke says that he doesn't like to lower himself," does not solve the problem. Whether such plot details are presented in the form of direct quotations or paraphrases, they are closed factual statements requiring no development. Such details may be used as evidence or illustration within a paragraph, but they cannot serve as the paragraph's main idea.

Here is the same paragraph with a topic sentence stating the interpretive point the writer wishes to make and setting up the development to follow:

> The duke's dissatisfaction with his late wife seems to have resulted from the conflict between her natural, innocent joy in living and the stern duke's "nine-hundred-years-old name." It is pathetically ironic that the duke never mentioned his unhappiness to his bride because "E'en then would be some stooping; and I choose / Never to stoop." The duke could not forgive his wife for not sharing his pride in his position. "She had / A heart," he says, "too soon made glad." The duchess seems to have had no sense of social superiority, a dangerously liberal attitude for one married to a man obsessed with his birth and position.

Paragraphs, whether in literary analysis or other types of writing, should never begin with illustrative details or closed statements (self-evident facts requiring no development). These come later, *after* you have stated the main idea that the factual details will illustrate. To put it simply, topic sentences in literary analysis papers should be *ideas* about the literature, not factual details from it.

51. TRANSITION

Use transitional words and phrases within paragraphs and between paragraphs.

1. Transition within paragraphs

> In a paragraph, each sentence should flow smoothly into the next one. Use transitional devices to show the relationship of your sentences and to avoid abrupt shifts in thought.

Paragraph lacking transition:

> The general public considers Robert Frost a simple, optimistic poet. There is a lot of pessimism in Frost's poetry. Poems like "Mowing" and "The Pasture" are romantic and optimistic. "Stopping by Woods on a Snowy Evening" seems to be a serene poem about a snowfall. The woods are "lovely, dark and deep." The poem has a weary tone. The speaker says that he has "miles to go before I sleep." "Design," "Desert Places," and "Acquainted with the Night" are pessimistic poems.

The same paragraph with transitions:

> The general public considers Robert Frost a simple, optimistic poet, *but* there is a lot of pessimism in his poetry. *While* a few of his poems, such as "Mowing" and "The Pasture," are romantic and optimistic, some look more romantic on the surface than they really are. "Stopping by Woods on a Snowy Evening," *for instance,* may seem to be a serene poem about a snowfall. The speaker describes the snow-filled woods as "lovely." *However,* he *also* says they are "dark and deep," both foreboding adjectives. *In addition,* the gloom of the poem is emphasized by its ending. *In this weary conclusion,* the speaker twice says that he has "miles to go before I sleep." *This image* of life as a long and tedious journey is hardly optimistic. *Other poems,* such as "Design," "Desert Places," and "Acquainted with the Night" are *even more* pessimistic.

Note that tying together the sentences of a paragraph with transition improves development as well as coherence.

2. Transition between paragraphs

In an essay, each paragraph should flow smoothly into the next one. Use transitional devices to show the relationship of your paragraphs and to avoid abrupt shifts in thought, as in these examples:

a. End of paragraph (classification of football fans):

This type of fan is a lot like the guy-next-door—if you live next door to Howard Cosell.

Beginning of the next paragraph:

While the Expert is mostly a harmless bore, the Drunk is physically dangerous.

Explanation: "While the Expert is mostly a harmless bore" points back to the character type just described; "Drunk" introduces the next character type.

b. End of paragraph (analysis of student rebellion in the sixties):

Many of these radicals simply lacked self-discipline.

Beginning of next paragraph:

Unlike these immature protestors, some were motivated by genuine idealism.

Explanation: "these immature protestors" points back to the radicals who lacked self-discipline; "genuine idealism" introduces the next topic.

c. End of paragraph (character sketch):

She was the weirdest teacher I'd ever had.

Beginning of next paragraph:

I soon learned that although Miss Hitop was odd, she really knew her subject.

Explanation: "although Miss Hitop was odd" refers back to "weirdest teacher"; "she really knew her subject" introduces the next trait.

d. End of paragraph (description):

The garish colors of the room created an effect of incredible tackiness.

Beginning of next paragraph:

The furnishings were just as tasteless.

Explanation: "just as tasteless" continues the idea of tackiness; "furnishings" introduces the next feature to be described.

e. End of paragraph (narrative):

There I was, standing beside my broken-down motorcycle on a lonely dirt road.

Beginning of next paragraph:

While I was trying to think of something to do, a black, hearselike car came around the bend and slowed to a stop beside me.

Explanation: "trying to think of something to do" refers back to standing beside the useless motorcycle; the appearance of the hearselike car introduces a shift in the action.

f. End of paragraph (short story analysis):

Such description emphasizes Phoenix's dignity and the importance of her journey.

Beginning of next paragraph:

> To complete this quest, Phoenix must overcome many obstacles.

Explanation: "this quest" refers back to "her journey"; "Phoenix must overcome many obstacles" introduces the main idea of the next paragraph.

Transitions are always subordinated to the main idea in a topic sentence. Transitions are useful guides for both reader and writer, but they are only functional and therefore do not deserve the emphasis of a separate sentence or even a main clause. Instead, transitions should be incorporated unobtrusively into topic sentences in the form of single words, phrases, or dependent clauses, as in the preceding examples.

52. UNGRAMMATICAL SENTENCE STRUCTURE

While such errors as comma splices and fragments make ungrammatical sentences, many sentences are nonstandard in less obvious ways. Ungrammatical sentences often make perfect sense, but they are not expressed in acceptable English form. They should be avoided because they create the impression of illiteracy. Here are some examples of ungrammatical sentences:

1.   In the poem "Richard Cory" shows how loneliness can lead to tragedy.

    Problem: "In the poem 'Richard Cory,'" an introductory prepositional phrase, is erroneously used as the subject of the verb "shows."

    Revision:

    > The poem "Richard Cory" shows how loneliness can lead to tragedy.

2.   Lila, she is just wonderful!

Problem: "Lila, she" is a redundant double subject.

Revision:

Lila is just wonderful!

3.   I just heard something terrible, which it is none of my business, but I want to tell you about it.

Problem: "which it" gives the adjective clause two subjects.

Revision:

I just heard something terrible, which is none of my business, but I want to tell you about it.

4.   Her son, of whom she was very proud of, was awarded the Bronze Star.

Problem: "of whom she was very proud of" has one preposition too many.

Revision:

Her son, whom she was very proud of, was awarded the Bronze Star.

Or:

Her son, of whom she was very proud, was awarded the Bronze Star.

5.   He asked me why would I do that.

Problem: The forms for direct and indirect questions are mixed together.

Revision:

He asked me why I would do that.

Or:

He asked me, "Why would you do that?"

6.   Tom wanted to be remembered and a success.

Problem: This sentence has a severe error in parallel structure.

Revision:

Tom wanted to succeed and to be remembered.

53. WORDINESS

Eliminate wasted words.

Good writers express their ideas as concisely as possible. The best sentence is not always the shortest one, but you should never use two words if the thought can be expressed as well in one. Don't waste words. Remove deadwood.

1. Wordy:

In "Ozymandias," Shelley's narrator deals with describing the ruins of an ancient land.

Concise:

In "Ozymandias," Shelley's narrator describes the ruins of an ancient land.

2. Wordy:

This company is built on the use of labor.

Concise:

This company is built on labor.

3. Wordy:

> I feel that you are using the excuse of bad luck to cover up your lack of initiative.

Concise:

> You are using bad luck to excuse your lack of initiative.

4. Wordy:

> The dress styles were dull and boring to him.

Concise:

> The dress styles bored him.

5. Wordy:

> At that point in time, I was not aware of the developments which were then taking place.

Concise:

> At the time, I didn't know what was going on.

6. Wordy:

> With regard to that matter, I can make no statement at this particular time.

Concise:

> No comment.

Most wordiness results from carelessly uneconomical expression or muddled thinking. Some wordiness, however, is the result of the writer's attempt to "pad out" a paper to a certain length or to sound "literary." This is the worst kind of overwriting. Don't do it.

Padded:

> As far as the much-discussed world of higher education is concerned, it is, in my opinion, fraught with abuses of the academic nature and in drastic need of innovative measures, which must be implemented in the immediate future on an ongoing basis.

Concise:

> The abuses of higher education must be remedied immediately.

Regardless of the type of paper you are writing, you will have plenty to say if you know your subject and if you supply supporting details and examples, discuss them, and relate them to the point you wish to make. If you communicate your thought clearly and thoroughly, you will not need to count words—or add them meaninglessly.

54. WORD ORDER

Place related words together in the sentence.

Words which go together in meaning should be placed as closely together in a sentence as the idiom of English syntax will allow.

1. Incorrect:

> The trophy is in the case which he won.

Revision:

> The trophy which he won is in the case.

2. Incorrect:

> He fouled the procedure up.

Revision:

He fouled up the procedure.

3. Incorrect:

   She talked about dying frequently.

   Revision:

   She frequently talked about dying.

4. Incorrect:

   I only have five minutes.

   Revision:

   I have only five minutes.

5. Incorrect:

   Proofread your papers before turning them in one last time.

   Revision:

   Proofread your papers one last time before turning them in.

55. WRONG WORDS

Choose grammatically correct word forms.

A "wrong word" is a severe diction error. While an error marked "diction" indicates an inexact word or phrase, a "wrong word" is the use of a nonstandard, ungrammatical expression. For instance, the use of "as" in the following sentence is an ungrammatical word choice—a wrong word:

He is not the lazy vagrant *as* some people take him to be.

The idiom of this sentence calls for "that," not "as":

He is not the lazy vagrant *that* some people take him to be.

If "as" is used, the sentence must be reconstructed:

He is not *as* lazy *as* some people think.

Some wrong words, such as "kinda," "heighth," "hisself," "theirselves," and "somewheres," are ungrammatical simply because they are nonwords. More common, however, is ungrammatical word choice resulting from the use of an incorrect word in place of another which is close to it in form or sound. Following are examples of "wrong word" errors. The correct form is in brackets:

1. Some people refuse to *except* [accept] reality.
2. I could *of* [have] passed if I had studied.
3. He doesn't do *nothing* [anything] for me.
4. I *can't* [can] hardly get up for my eight o'clock class.
5. The new law does not *effect* [affect] me.
6. I felt the *affects* [effects] of the new law.
7. A new law was *affected* [effected] by the state legislature.
8. The reason you have trouble is *because* [that] you don't listen.
9. Divide the money *between* [among] all the workers.
10. Hager is the man *which* [who] is responsible. ("Who" refers to people, "which" to things, and "that" to either people or things.)
11. I'm going to *lay* [lie] out in the sun today. ("Lay" means "to place," as in "Lay the book on my desk."

"Lie" means to recline, as in "Lie down and rest." The past tense of "lie," however, is "lay," as in "I lay down for an hour yesterday afternoon.")

12. *Set* [sit] down and rest awhile. ("Sit," like "lie," refers to body positioning. "Set," like "lay," means "to place," as in "Set the milk bottles on the porch.")

13. Today's students are different *than* [from] those of a decade ago.

14. The team played *good* [well] yesterday. (Except with "sense" words such as "feel," "smell," and "taste," the word "good" cannot be used as a modifier following a verb.)

   a. The following sentences are correct:

     I feel good today.

     That perfume smells good.

     Steak always tastes good to me.

   But compare:

     Taste it well to get the full flavor.

   b. In most sentences, the adverb "well" is the correct modifier form:

     I hope to get a well-paying job.

     You did well on your test.

     Speak louder—I don't hear well.

     I missed the knockout because I was behind a post and couldn't see well.

15. The team played *bad* [badly]. (The adverb "badly" and not the adjective "bad" is required to modify a verb. In this sentence, "badly" modifies the verb "played.")

After such special verbs as "look," "taste," and "feel," however, the adjective "bad" is correct:

You really look bad this morning.

That soup tastes bad.

I don't feel bad about my grammar now.

(Acknowledgments continued from page vi)

permission of editor. Quotations from "Can We Predict the Coming California Quake?," by George Alexander, are used by permission of *Popular Science Monthly*. Quotations from "A Worn Path" in *A Curtain of Green and Other Stories*, by Eudora Welty, are used by permission of Harcourt Brace Jovanovich, Inc.; copyright 1941, 1969 by Eudora Welty. Quotations from "Miniver Cheevy" in *The Town Down the River*, by E.A. Robinson, are used by permission of Charles Scribner's Sons; copyright 1907 Charles Scribner's Sons; renewal copyright 1938 Ruth Nivison. Quotations from "The Mill" in *Collected Poems* of Edwin Arlington Robinson are used by permission of Macmillan Publishing Co., Inc.; copyright 1920 by Edwin Arlington Robinson; renewed 1948 by Ruth Nivison. Quotations from *Deliverance*, by James Dickey, are used by permission of Houghton Mifflin Company; copyright ©1970 by James Dickey.

Index

387

course titles, 276
days of week, 275
family relationship terms, 276
first word of dialogue, 277
first word of sentence, 275
geographical directions and
    names, 276
holidays, 275
I, 275
ideological words not
    capitalized, 277
languages, 276
names of groups, 276–77
names of months, 275
occupational terms, 276
periods of time, 275
place-names, 275
poetry quotations, 267, 278,
    298–99
proper names, 275
prose quotations, 277
seasons not capitalized, 276
subjects of study, 276
in titles, 277
Card catalog, 116–18
Case, pronoun, 336–38
in comparisons, 337
of compound objects, 337
with gerunds, 338
nominative, 336
objective, 336
possessive, 337
of *who* and *whom*, 337–38
Character sketch themes,
    74–84
description and prewriting,
    74–75

dominant characteristics, use
    of, 74
organization, 74
sample essays, 75–83
sample topics, 84
selectivity, 74
style, 74–75
Choppiness, 278–79
Classification themes, 34–42
description and prewriting,
    34–36
label names, 36
organization, 35–36
overlapping categories, 35
parallelism of types, 36
sample essay, 36–41
sample topics, 41–42
selectivity, 35
stereotyping, 34
Clichés, 279–80
Collective nouns, 335, 356–57
Colons, 280–82, 348
after elliptical introductions,
    281
after greeting in business
    letters, 281–82
after introductory
    statements, 280–81
not after introductory
    phrases or clauses, 281
with quotation marks, 348
Comma faults. *See* Comma
    splices
Commas, 281, 282–87, 291, 348
in pairs, 283, 284, 285
with coordinating
    conjunctions connecting

Marking Symbols